The Six Scrolls

of the

Revelations Grid

by Roxanne Tonkin

ISBN-978-1-7320169-4-1

LCCN-2018901887

CONTENTS

NOTES:

NOTES:

CHAPTER 1 — PRESUPPOSITIONS

Looking backward, into the deepest recorded histories of mankind, we find that there was a definitive moment in time — prearranged by God — when He would begin a miraculous amendment to His broken creation. Mankind had indeed been broken in the Garden — but the Creator who loved us (too much, to lose us) had orchestrated an elaborate and infallible plan to rescue us from our brokenness. The only thing mankind would have to bring to the table, was faith.

With His perfect salvation plan already in place before Adam was created, God was waiting and ready to catch Adam when he fell (foreknowing all things). There, God began patiently tutoring fallen mankind through the generations — awaiting the moment when the hope of mankind would finally evolve into the level of faith that was necessary for His plan to begin in earnest. And soon, it did — through the extraordinary heart of a man named Abraham (the first to be called a 'Hebrew' [meaning; 'one set apart']).

Through faithful Abraham, God would eventually grow and establish an entire nation of people He would call His own; the Hebrew tribe called 'Israel'. It was to Israel that God would impart the first half of His glorious amendment to humanity; the first 'Word' (or, 'Witness') of God's testimony to mankind. And, just like that; Israel would be christened God's 'prepared-example' to all of mankind.

This First Word/Witness revealed to mankind what is broken inside us — and, that we are condemned to die if that which is broken is not fixed. This knowledge was revealed to Israel through the Word of the 'Law'; which taught mankind that we are utterly corrupted in sin, but did nothing to strengthen us to rise above that sin. Thank goodness that first Word/Witness also promised God would eventually send us a second Word/Witness (the last half of God's amendment), which would provide to us the missing component (the strength/means) that would make it possible for us to overcome our deficiency. This promise (the foretelling of the second Word/Witness to come) was revealed to Israel through the Word of 'Prophecy'. Thus; God's first amendment to mankind (first Word/Witness) consists of Law and Prophecy — and it has been canonized as the 'Old Testament' Bible.

That First Word/amendment was the first of two Witnesses God would ultimately send into the earth to provide His testimony to mankind — and it was delivered to Israel (who is called God's 'first-born' son). This first Word/Witness was an amendment to the will (which is rooted in the mind; 'will' being the spirit-aspect of 'soul'). This first amendment was purposed to bring one's will back into submission to, and reverence of, God's will—(i.e.; it was purposed to bring about repentance). Water Baptism is the outward (physical) sacrament associated with this inward (spiritual) repentance.

The outward testimony of Water Baptism—(i.e.; the cleansing of the physical-aspect of soul) is every bit as required as the inward repentance—(i.e.; the cleansing of the spirit-aspect of soul). Jesus acknowledged that even he had to Water Baptize his (condemned) flesh to fulfill 'all' righteousness (Matt 3:15 & John 3:6). Repentant Water Baptism restores the willing servant (the vessel; will + body). But, again; this first amendment doesn't plant within us the substance that can manifest the essence of God from within us — that second part of His amendment would come later.

As man's new-found understanding (and acceptance) of God's will trickled down through the generations of Israel, thereafter, it was brilliantly·camouflaged from the Serpent by the thousands of souls that made up the nation of Israel. For centuries, the children of Israel tried (and failed, in large part) to attain to perfection before the Law of God. Man was, after all, human. Nevertheless; God's provisions of mercy and patience would offer many bandaids to preserve Israel's anointing, in spite of their human weakness. Ironically, it was that very rollercoaster that would eventually bring all of humanity to the undeniable conviction that mankind cannot possibly attain to perfection simply by 'knowing' God's rules. Thus, it had finally become effectual for God to send us His second (last) amendment; the 'substance' we lacked (to become the whole image/likeness of God).

The second (last) amendment in God's salvation plan required Him to impregnate prepared-Israel with the Seed of His Holy Spirit of Truth, so that His Son (likeness) could be born into the world inside of a human body (finally returning to mankind the Holy-substance which was lost in the Garden of Eden). In other words; Christ the Son was sent into the world to personally deliver the Last Word (which had been promised to us by the First Word).

This last Word/Witness would be the story (or, testimony) of the life and willing death of Jesus Christ, the Son of God (whose death paid the sin-debt owed by mankind because of Adam's fall) and the reward of resurrection and eternal life for accomplishing that willing sacrifice. This Word/Witness has been canonized (together with the writings of the Apostles) as the 'New Testament' Bible. (It has been argued that many of the currently uncanonized apocrypha should also be included as part of this last amendment.) Nevertheless; the first amendment to mankind had been the Law (which defined our condemnation) and the Prophecy (which promised to save us from that condemnation) — and the second (last) amendment to mankind was the literal manifestation of that promised salvation-mechanism (Jesus Christ, the Messiah; who, brought back to us the Seed of the Holy Spirit of Truth). Willingly, Jesus accomplished this deed; being born into the prison of human flesh, growing up amid temptation and evil, and successfully paying the full debt owed by mankind, for sin — successfully bringing back into the world the nourishing strength/means (the heart-substance) we needed to rise above our sinful nature, going forward.

This last Word/Witness was the second of two Witnesses God ultimately sent into the earth to provide His testimony (or, amendment) to mankind — and it entered the world through Jesus (who is called God's 'only-begotten' son). This was an amendment of the 'substance' (of the heart/goodness of man) — unlike the first amendment, which had been an amendment to the 'will' (of the mind of man). This heart-amendment/substance is the Seed of the Holy Spirit of Truth; which, alone, restores Goodness [the heart of man]. True/eternal Goodness was the intended spiritual 'husband' of our spiritual soul/will; Goodness + Will = Good-Will. But this is only possible if Goodness is awake/alive. This last amendment plants the Holy Seed of God back into our heart/Goodness again, restoring the 'enlivened' husband to the Bride; restoring in us the one-and-only substance which can manifest God's essence from within us; true and eternal goodness. This (the Holy Spirit of Truth) was the inner-substance that Adam & Eve lost in the Garden of Eden. Now, Goodness and Will would be reunited again so that good-will (the Holy Estate/marriage) replaces free-will (see; Luke 2:10-14). This was how mankind was intended to exist from the beginning; with Goodness in charge, rather than unbridled Will.

Together, these two Words (of the Holy Spirit) are the 'Two Witnesses' of God's testimony on earth; the first and last amendments sent to restore mankind to his Creator (His first and last covenants with mankind)—(See; Fig. 1 [pg. 14]). These Two Witnesses are the two halves that produce a whole (redeemable) image/likeness of God. In other words; a man's soul must embrace (and profess) both Witnesses,

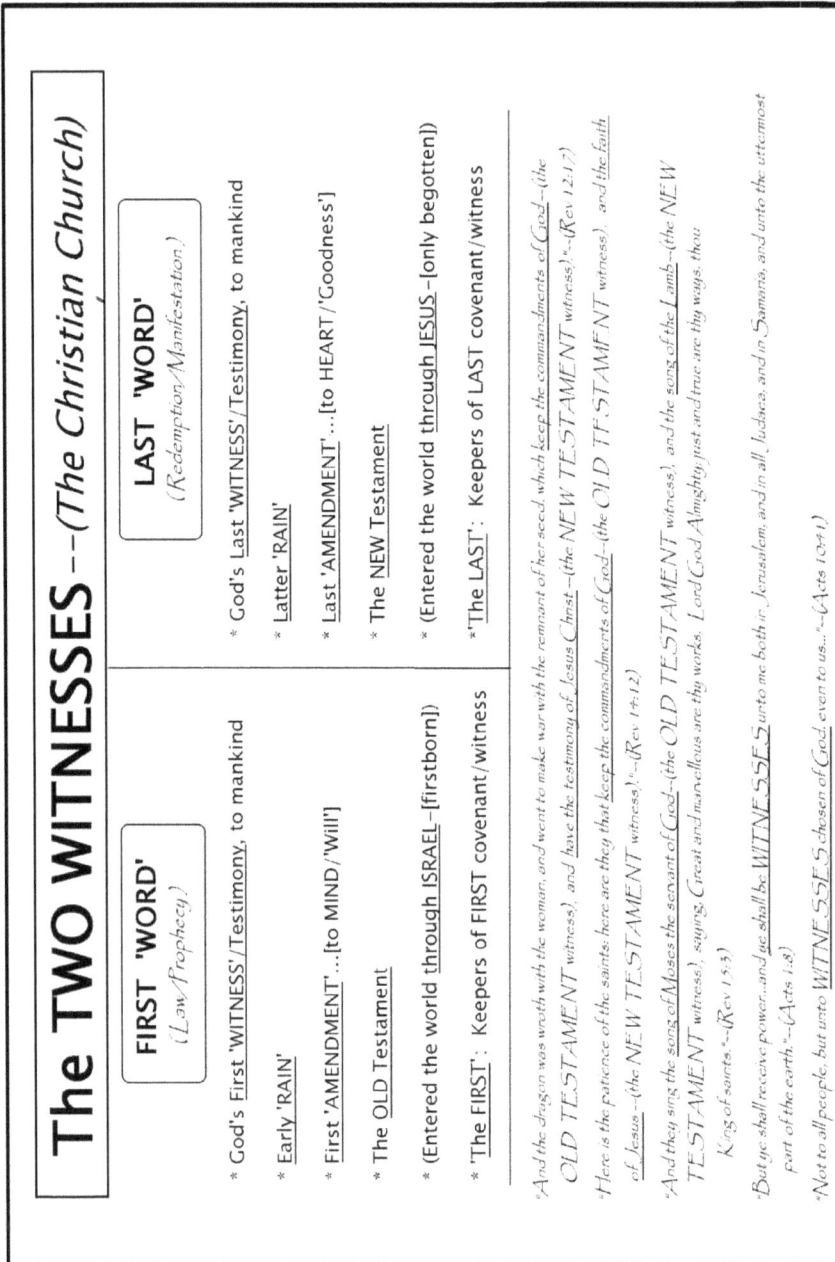

The TWO WITNESSES --(The Christian Church)

FIRST 'WORD'
(Law/Prophecy)

* God's First 'WITNESS'/Testimony, to mankind
* Early 'RAIN'
* First 'AMENDMENT'...[to MIND/'Will']
* The OLD Testament
* (Entered the world through ISRAEL-[firstborn])
* 'The FIRST': Keepers of FIRST covenant/witness

LAST 'WORD'
(Redemption/Manifestation)

* God's Last 'WITNESS'/Testimony, to mankind
* Latter 'RAIN'
* Last 'AMENDMENT'...[to HEART/'Goodness']
* The NEW Testament
* (Entered the world through JESUS-[only begotten])
* 'The LAST': Keepers of LAST covenant/witness

"And the dragon was wroth with the woman, and went to make war with the remnant of her seed, which keep the commandments of God--(the OLD TESTAMENT witness), and have the testimony of Jesus Christ--(the NEW TESTAMENT witness)."--(Rev 12:17)

"Here is the patience of the saints: here are they that keep the commandments of God--(the OLD TESTAMENT witness), and the faith of Jesus--(the NEW TESTAMENT witness)."--(Rev 14:12)

"And they sing the song of Moses the servant of God--(the OLD TESTAMENT witness), and the song of the Lamb--(the NEW TESTAMENT witness), saying, Great and marvellous are thy works, Lord God Almighty; just and true are thy ways, thou King of saints."--(Rev 15:3)

"But ye shall receive power...and ye shall be WITNESSES unto me both in Jerusalem, and in all Judaea, and in Samaria, and unto the uttermost part of the earth."--(Acts 1:8)

"Not to all people, but unto WITNESSES chosen of God, even to us..."--(Acts 10:41)

(Fig. 1 -- The Two Witnesses)

to be fully amended; this completion is what makes any

particular soul a part of the Body of Christ. It was

in fact Christ the Son (existing with God, in Heaven,

even before the world began) who 'spoke' both the Old
Testament Word and the New Testament Word into the
world. However; Christ the Son didn't inhabit a
physical body until he was born inside of the baby
Jesus (Jesus + Christ = Jesus-Christ). In Revelation
1:11, the risen Jesus Christ said; *"I am the first
(Word/Witness) and the last (Word/Witness)."* Consider
the following verses, which reflect the natural (and
dependent) association of these two
'Words'/amendments:

> *(Ref: Rev 12:17)*—*"And the Dragon was wroth with
> the Woman, and went to make war with the Remnant
> of her seed, which keep the commandments of God
> (the Old Testament Word), and have the testimony
> of Jesus Christ (the New Testament Word)."*
> And...
> *(Ref: Rev 14:12)*—*"Here is the patience of the
> saints: here are they that keep the commandments
> of God (the Old Testament Witness), and the faith
> of Jesus (the New Testament Witness)."*
> And...
> *(Ref: Rev 15:3)*—*"And they-(the resurrected
> Christian-Witnesses) sing the song of Moses the*

servant of God (the Old Testament Word), *and* (they sing) *the song of the Lamb* (the New Testament Word)..."

And...

(Ref: Acts 1:8)—"But ye-(the Christianized apostles) *shall receive power* (Holy Spirit)*...and ye shall be Witnesses unto me both in Jerusalem, and in all Judaea, and in Samaria, and unto the uttermost part of the earth."*

And...

(Ref: Acts 10:41)—"Not to all people (was the risen Jesus revealed), *but unto Witnesses chosen of God, even to us-*(the Christianized apostles)."

The Word of God is saturated with promises to mankind. Perhaps most amazingly of all, is that each Word (Testament) guarantees mankind that if we never walk away from them (the Words of God) they will convict our heart and bring about our salvation — guaranteed! The first Word-(Old Testament) promises that as long as we are willing to read and meditate on it (daily), the Old Testament will lead us directly to the feet of Jesus (the New Testament). And the Last Word-(New Testament) promises that as long as we are willing to read and meditate on it (daily), the New Testament will fill us with all the faith required to guarantee our salvation.

Public Communion-('partaking' of the Lord's body) is the outward (physical) sacrament associated with this daily inward (spiritual) consumption of the Word/scripture-(Bread-from-Heaven). This outward (physical) testimony of Communion — 'displaying' the purpose of Jesus' life and death — is every bit as required as the daily (spiritual) intake of God's Word/Bread. Jesus set this example for us at the Last Supper when he instructed his followers to present this outward testimony to the world to 'show' the Lord's death (sacrifice) until he returns (1 Cor 11:26). Worthy Communion strengthens (and projects) the child of God within us. In other words; it restores the 'lively' heart of man; the flow of His spirit coming into and going out of us). 'Worthy' (in the previous sentence) simply implies 'with a clean conscience'; having no unconfessed sin in your soul at the time that you are partaking or projecting. If there is unconfessed-sin in your soul, neither effort will have the life-sustaining effect they were designed to produce. Consider the verses below, which reflect the promises attached to ingesting the Word of God (daily):

>*(Ref: Rom 10:17)—"So then faith comes by hearing* (the Word)*, and hearing* (comes) *by the word of God* (the scripture)*."*

And...

>*(Ref: John 6:44)—"No man can come to me-*(Jesus)*, except the Father* (Spirit of Truth) *which has sent me draw him* (to me)*: and I will raise him-*(the follower of Truth) *up at the last day."*

And...

>*(Ref: John 6:37)—"All that the Father gives me* (every soul that the Spirit of Truth leads to the promised Messiah) *shall come to me* (shall find me)*; and him that cometh to me* (the child who embraces Truth) *I will in no wise cast out."*

In the end times; when the Two Witnesses (indwelling Christianized-mankind) are harvested from the Earth, 144,000 (devout) Jews will have their eyes opened to Jesus by the miraculous events of that harvest. Those 144,000 will finally recognize and accept Jesus Christ as the 'Messiah' promised to

mankind by the First Word-(Old Testament Prophecy).
Because these final converts do not yet believe in
Jesus at the moment this harvest begins, they won't be
able to be harvested with the Christianized church-
(the 'Two Witnesses'). These 144,000 will have to stay
on Earth and endure the Tribulations-Period-(the Seven
Last Plagues of Wrath) before finally being harvested
by God (at Jesus' Second Coming). The Revelation of
John — when correctly aligned and interpreted —
clearly depicts these two separate harvest events
during the seven-year-period preceding the 1,000-Year-
Reign. The following verse alludes to the two separate
end-time harvest events (harvests of souls who must be
in covenant with 'both' Witnesses, to be harvested):

> (Ref: Matt 19:30)—"Many that are first (covenant)
> shall be last (harvested)—(i.e.; the
> 144,000/Remnant of Israel); and the last
> (covenant)—(i.e.; the Innumerable multitudes of
> Christian-Witnesses) shall be (harvested) first."

Throughout the entire salvation plan (from Adam,
to the 1,000-Year-Reign) there are a total of three
'harvests' of God's anointed people. The first time of
harvest is frequently overlooked; it took place

immediately after the resurrection of Jesus himself (2000+ years ago, when the souls of 'many of the saints which slept' [Matt 27:52] were resurrected from their graves, walked the Earth [as Jesus did], and were raised to the Sea of Glass under the altar of God [Rev 6:9-11]). The three harvests of anointed mankind are referred to in scripture as; the 'time', 'times' & 'dividing of time' (as mentioned in verses such as those noted below):

(Ref: Rev 12:14)—"And to the Woman-(mankind; the intended Bride of Christ) *were given two wings of a great eagle* (Old Testament Word & New Testament Word), *that she might fly into the wilderness-*(place of ungodliness), *into her place, where she is nourished for a time, and times, and half a time,* (away) *from the face of the Serpent—*(i.e.; until all three harvests are completed)."

And...

(Ref: Dan 7:25)—"And they-(God's people) *shall be given into his-*(Satan's) *hand until a time and times and the dividing of time—*(i.e.; until all three harvests are completed)."

And...

(Ref: Eph 1:10)—"That in the dispensation of the fullness of times (i.e.; after the completion of all three harvests) *he*-(Christ) *might gather together in one all things in Christ, both which are in heaven* (on the Sea of Glass), *and which are on earth, even in him—*(i.e.; gathering us all into the single Body of Christ)."

And...

(Ref: Luke 13:30)—"And, behold, there are last (covenant) *which shall be* (harvested) *first—* (i.e.; Christians) *and there are first* (covenant) *which shall be* (harvested) *last—*(i.e.; the Remnant of Israel/144,000)."

In the above verses, 'time' refers to the harvest of the Early-Saints, 'times' refers to the harvest of the Christian-Witnesses, and the 'dividing of time' (or, the 'half a Time') refers to the harvest of a fractional Remnant of Israel (the 144,000 last Remnant). — (See; Fig. 2 [pg. 22])

According to the Revelation of John, the Christian-Witnesses (the fleshen-vessels indwelled by the Two-Witnesses) will be killed and resurrected (to the Sea of Glass) at the end of a 3.5-year period

THREE 'HARVESTS' of Annointed Children

a 'TIME'	'TIMES'	a 'dividing' of TIME
* The EARLY SAINTS	* The TWO WITNESSES	* The 144,000/Remnant
* (Raised at Jesus' resurrection)	* (Resurrected at the 6th TRUMP)	* (Resurrected/'CHANGED' at the 7th PLAGUE)
* Under the altar of God at 5th SEAL	* The 'FIRST' [end-time] 'harvest'	* The 'LAST' [end-time] 'harvest'

"And he shall speak great words against the most High, and shall wear out the saints of the most High, and think to change times and laws: and they shall be given into his hand until a TIME, and TIMES and the DIVIDING OF TIME."—(Dan 7:25)

"And to the woman—(Collective SOUL of mankind) were given two wings of a great eagle—(two WORDS of God), that she might fly into the wilderness, into her place, where she is nourished for a TIME, and TIMES and HALF a TIME, from the face of the serpent."—(Rev 12:14)

"And behold, there are last—(CHRISTIANS) which shall be [harvested] first, and there are first—(Remnant [of ISRAEL] /144,000]) which shall be [harvested] last."—(Luk 13:30)

"That in the dispensation of the fulness of TIMES [of harvest] he might gather together in one, all things in Christ, both which are in heaven, and which are on earth; even in him."—(Eph 1:10)

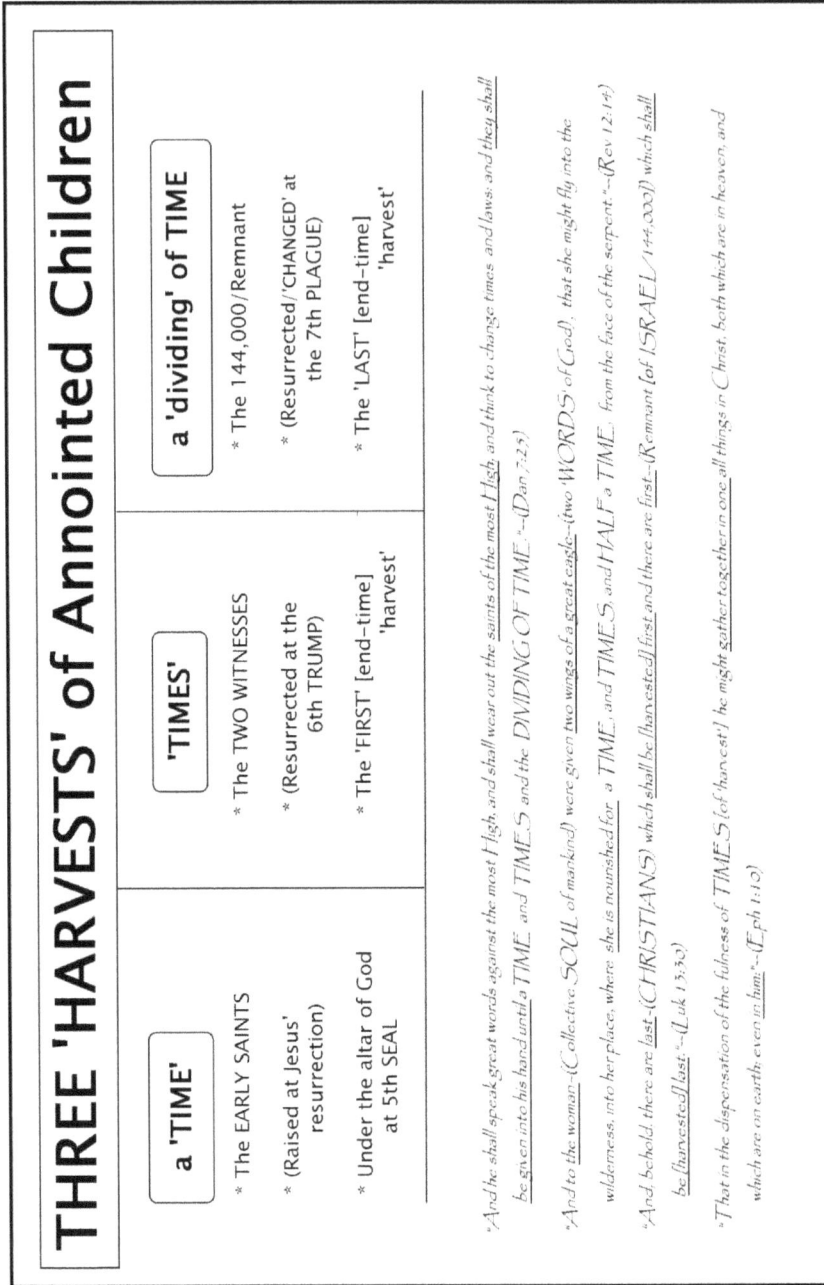

(Fig. 2: Three Harvests of Anointed Children)

called the 'Beginning of Sorrows' (aka; the 'Sorrows-Period'). That period will be immediately followed by a second 3.5-year period called the 'Tribulations-

Period'-(the Seven Last Plagues of Wrath), which will end when the Risen Jesus slays/immortalizes the 144,000/Remnant of Israel (ushering them into the 1,000-Year Reign). In other words; the Christian-Witnesses will be harvested halfway through the 7-year Sorrows/Tribulations-Period — but, the 144,000/Remnant (of Israel) will not be harvested until the end of that seven-year-period. I believe this 'dual-harvest' scenario is what accounts for Christianity's confusion about when (exactly) the 'rapture' will take place (in relation to the Tribulations-Period/Seven Last Plagues).

At the end of the Sorrows-Period, the Whore-(collective-soul of mankind that blasphemes Truth/Goodness; preferring the convenience of Error/Evil) who, is indwelled by the Beast-(Legions of Error/Evil-[the dark angels]) will rise up against the current Kingdom of God (the Christian-Witnesses/Two-Witnesses]) and overcome them (killing every Christian on the face of the Earth). Three days later, Jesus will call the (slain) souls of those Christian-Witnesses up into Heaven; harvesting them from the Earth. Afterward; Jesus will actually come back into the Earth (his 'Second Coming') to unleash the Tribulations-Period-(Seven Last Plagues of Wrath) — at the end of which, he will kill every Whore-soul on the face of the Earth, and then slay/immortalize the 144,000/Remnant of Israel (ushering them into the 1,000-Year-Reign, on Earth).

This would probably be a good time to address the worldly use of the word 'rapture' in end-time discussions. The word 'rapture' doesn't actually appear anywhere in the scriptures, and I would personally hesitate to call either of these two end-time harvests a rapture (which implies 'blissful'). The Lord, himself, will harvest the 144,000/Remnant in the 'twinkling of an eye' (slaying them, with His sword); rescuing them from the violence and insanity of the Tribulations-Period-(the Seven Last Plagues of Wrath). However; they will already have endured the full 3.5-year Sorrows-Period and the full 3.5-year Tribulations-Period. (I suppose death, itself, might seem blissful at that point.) And, true; the harvest of the Christian-Witnesses will occur after having endured only the 3.5-year Sorrows-Period — but, their deaths will be at the hands of an angry, hateful mob (whereas the 144,000/Remnant will at least die by the merciful sword of a Loving Savior). Even the 'many saints who slept' (who were resurrected during Jesus' resurrection, as stated in Matt 27:52) were said to have been 'killed' for the sake of the Lord (as martyrs). In any event, 'Harvest' seems a more honest word for these events, to my mind.

Another presupposition I've arrived at over the years is that the world-wide annihilation of the Christian-Witnesses (the Two Witnesses) will almost certainly be the event that reveals the 'man of sin'. Literally speaking; who else but sinful mankind would kill all Christians on the Earth? It also makes sense to me that the complete elimination of the power/presence of the Holy-Seed from Earth (at that time) is what the Bible refers to when it mentions a 'great falling away' (of Christians) which will precede Jesus' Second Coming. Again, literally speaking; all Christians will have been wiped off the face of the Earth. (I'm referring to the precursors mentioned in the following verses):

(Ref: 2 Thes 2:3)—"Let no man deceive you by any means: for that day (the Second Coming of Jesus)

shall not come, except there come a falling away

first (of Kingdom of God)*, and that Man of Sin*

(ungodly man) *be revealed, the son of perdition-*

(the world)*;"*

And...

(Ref: Rev 11:7)—"When they-(the Christian-

Witnesses/Two-Witnesses) *shall have finished*

their testimony, the Beast-(Legions of

Error/Evil) *that ascends out of the Bottomless*

Pit shall make war against them, and shall

overcome them, and kill them."

This makes sense when we review the events in

their proper order: First; Evil finally makes a move

to annihilate the (entire) Kingdom of God—(i.e.; the

Whore-Movement of the Sorrows-Period). Then; Jesus

must respond (by coming to Earth with his army to

destroy the Whore).

Equally important in understanding the

'Revelation of John' as a whole, is the very clear

distinction that exists between 'the Woman', 'the

Bride', and 'the Whore' mentioned in the Revelation.

If Jesus (the bridegroom) is intended to be mankind's

husband, then (clearly) humans are 'the Woman' whose

fidelity is at issue, before God. With that in mind, let's examine the various faces of mankind (the Woman).

If 'the Woman' is the collective-soul of mankind (in general), and 'the Bride' is the collective-soul of mankind that 'marries' Jesus Christ (willing to breed Truth/Goodness into the world), then it stands to reason that 'the Whore' must be the collective-soul of mankind that 'marries' Satan/Legion (willing to breed Error/Evil into the world). The Bride-of-Christ becomes the 'mouth' of God, on Earth—(i.e.; the Prophet who speaks the voice of Truth/Christ). Likewise; the bride-of-Satan/Legion becomes the 'mouth' of Satan, on Earth—(i.e.; the False-Prophet who speaks the voice of Error/Antichrist). This leaves only the collective-soul of the 'Lukewarm'-mindset unaffiliated. The conclusions drawn above support the foundational understanding that Good is the opposite of Evil, Truth is the opposite of Error, and Christ is the opposite of Antichrist.

It is just as important to understand the role of the Lukewarm-mindset in the end-time scenarios, as it is to understand the role of the Bride and the Whore (outlined above). Able to make no sense of the notion of committing one's (free-will) allegiance to the authority of a partner/boss — either Truth or Error; God or Devil — the Lukewarm-mindset reverences only 'Self'-(the mortal soul) and professes that every individual should be allowed to do whatever makes them happy, as long as they don't infringe on someone else's right to accomplish the same. Willing to depend solely on her own (corruptible) logic as a life-guide, the Lukewarm-soul will be blown about by every wind of doctrine (conceding; only if/when forced to, by majority-rule).

Conversely; the Bride and the Whore have (willingly) entered into committed-lifestyle partnerships. The Whore-mindset reverences Error/Evil (and will readily ravage whomever and whatever necessary to achieve their own comfort and pleasure — with little concern for the souls/lives they effect). Committed to depend solely on survival-instinct as a life-guide, the Whore has willingly made herself the polar opposite of Truth and Goodness-(God). The Bride (of Christ), on the other hand, reverences Truth and Goodness (and is committed to replenishing the [willful] Earth with the Good/loving Spirit of God; growing the Kingdom of God). Committed to depend solely on Good-conscience as a guide, the Bride will emerge victorious and be rewarded with eternal life.

There is a similar distinction to be made between 'the Devil', 'the Beast', and 'the Antichrist' — but first, we need to acknowledge the undeniable correlation between Evil and Error. As we concluded in the paragraphs above; Good is the opposite of Evil, Truth is the opposite of Error, and Christ is the opposite of Antichrist. Many theologians aren't comfortable with Evil (the Devi l) sometimes being called 'Error' (because it suggests the two words are synonymous with each other). But, with those particular ear-plugs in, much available understanding would be lost to us.

It is by no means a mistake to use the two words interchangeably, here. Begin by thinking of Truth in the shape of a pie: When all the pieces (all the facts) are together in the pan, you have the 'whole' Truth-(the Holy Truth; the mind of God). If you remove just one piece of the pie (just one fact of Truth) you can no longer call that pie 'Truth'-(complete knowledge/wisdom); it has now become 'Error'-(partial-truth [the mirror-image of the Devil's mind]). We know that 'Goodness' means 'righteousness' (or, 'right'-ness). A thing cannot be right if part of it is missing/wrong. Thus, God exists in a state of Truth-(whole/right/goodness), whereas; the Devil exists in a state of Error-(incomplete/wrong/evil). The Tree of the Knowledge of Good and Evil produces some fruits of true knowledge and some fruits of erroneous/incomplete knowledge — whereas, the Tree of Life produces only fruits of true knowledge.

Now we can discuss the distinction that exists between the Devil, the Beast and the Antichrist. The 'Devil' is the Father of all Error/Evil-(Satan/Lucifer/Serpent). The 'Beast' is the collective-Legion of Error/Evil (the Legion of dark [ignorant] angels that serve at the Devil's pleasure). Like the Devil himself, the origin of these angels is currently the Abyss (the Pit). From there, they have the power to indwell any Whore-soul who commits to (or, embraces) a lifestyle-partnership with them. Likewise, this Legion has the power to influence Lukewarm souls (because these souls have no strength to resist them; having never made Jesus-[Truth/Goodness] the ruler of their heart, to strengthen and protect them from the influence of Error/Evil). The Beast-(Legions of Error/Evil) can actively participate among mankind only 'through' the ungodly souls who are willing to embrace and act out their evil desires. Prior to Jesus' victory, the Devil and his dark angels were able to roam the face of the Earth doing whatever they pleased.

My understanding of 'indwelling' spirits (good or evil), is this: When a human soul dies (goes to sleep), her spiritual-husband (the indwelling spirit) separates from the dead/sleeping soul and returns to his place of origin (whether Heaven or Hell). Spirits are fully able to influence any soul that is willing to partner with them in a deed — either, for a mutually-agreeable 'moment of weakness' (as with an 'influencing' spirit), or; for a mutually beneficial 'committed-lifestyle' of corruption (as with an 'indwelling' spirit-husband). Nevertheless; every human soul will be reunited to her chosen spirit-husband in the resurrection at the end of time. This is why every living soul is required to make a free-will choice between God and Satan.

The 'Antichrist' is the Voice of Error/Evil (speaking from the [incomplete/dim] mind of the Devil). The Antichrist-(Voice of Error) speaks through the mouths of the Whore-souls and Lukewarm-souls (False Prophets, by extension) whom they influence or indwell. For comparison, consider the opposite case; the Christ: The Christ is the Voice of Truth/Goodness (speaking from the [whole/Holy] mind of God). The man 'Jesus' was the 'mouth' through whom the Christ spoke, on Earth. Likewise; the Christ now speaks through the mouths of all Christian souls-(the Bride).

Today and in the end-time, the 'Christ' is the Voice of Truth/Goodness, pouring God's thoughts through the mouths of the Bride-(Prophets, by extension) — and, the 'Antichrist' is the Voice of Error/Evil, pouring the Devil's thoughts through the mouths of the Whore and Lukewarm souls-(False Prophets, by extension). The Antichrist is not a person (as many people have come to believe); it is the (ignorant) Voice of erroneous jargon (lacking knowledge/wisdom/light/Truth of God). The Antichrist is a spirit which lives 'through' many people — just as the spirit of Christ lives through many people. Identifying and correctly arranging the players on the field will take us a long way toward understanding the book of Revelation.

In the Revelation, the Whore-(collective-bride of Error/Evil) rides the Beast-(her husband; the Legions of Error/Evil) into world power; crushing whomever they please in their joint-endeavor to dominate and reign in the Earth. In the battle between good and evil, it isn't the job of godly mankind to kill the Whore or the Beast — it is our job to remove ourselves out from among them (away from their darkness and ignorance) by filling ourselves (and others) with the light/knowledge/Wisdom (Truth) of God. This job we must do; even at the cost of our own lives (which brings me to the next important mystery we need to unravel: What [or, who] is the 'Daily Sacrifice'?).

We should begin searching for the meaning of 'Daily Sacrifice' where it was first clearly defined for us, by God: In Old Testament Law, the Daily Sacrifice consisted of two sacrifices; the morning-sacrifice and the evening-sacrifice (the daily 'sinatonements'). When Christ the Son entered into the world and sacrificed himself for all mankind (Jews and Gentiles, alike; as per New Testament), his broken body replaced the former Daily Sacrifice defined by God (which had been a temporary example; to familiarize us with the sacrificial-lamb that would come later; Jesus Christ). When Jesus was willingly crucified, he (the Son of God) became the 'Passover-lamb' for all of humanity; Jews and Gentiles, alike (according to God's salvation plan, from the foundation of the world; foreknowing all things). Since then (and to this day), the Body of Christ remains the only 'sanctified' Daily Sacrifice—(i.e.; our only means of redemption). In the end-time, 144,000 souls of Israel will be seen as 'blameless virgins' (in God's eyes) under the Law of His first covenant. Nevertheless, the Revelation states that even their redemption will require the (atoning) blood of Jesus, to accomplish. Understanding these important presuppositions will make many other aspects of the Revelation fall effortlessly into place.

Perhaps the most challenging presupposition to embrace, will be; what (or, who) does the Revelation refer to when it speaks of the '3rd Part/Generation', the '4th Part/Generation', the '6th Part' and the '10th Part'. I believe it will become clear through our discussion that each and every time the 3rd Part is mentioned in the book of Revelation, the text is referring to vessels (or, 'bodies') that possess the anointed life-force-energy/power of God (whatever else '3rd Part' may imply). This will include his anointed people, as well as other anointed bodies in creation (such as celestial, etc...; wherein, scripture suggests that God may be storing reserves for use in the end time [1 Cor 15:39-41, 2 Pet 3:7 & Job 38:22-23]). Why, exactly, Jesus uses the words '3rd Part' in these instances remains a mystery to me (although, it appears to be related to the 3rd Seal). And where we see biblical references to the '3rd Generation', they too are referring to the anointed 3rd Part. This will make more sense if we can think of the word 'generation' in terms of the timing of a particular generation of energy (being generated) rather than as generations of family lineages.

Similarly, I believe it will become clear through our discussion that when the Revelation mentions the

'4th Part (or, generation)', it is a reference to the 4th Kingdom on Earth; the days of the empowered Whores of the three Whore-Movements against the Kingdom of God. These three Whore-Movements are 'Gog' (whatever else 'Gog' may imply). In like manner; when Old Testament scripture mentions the '6th Part', we will discover this is a reference to the Lukewarm (self-worshipping) souls that inhabit the Earth through the Tribulations-Period and the 1,000-Year-Reign. The '6th Part' is 'Magog'; the Lukewarm-mindset (whatever else 'Magog' may imply).

The first Whore-Movement against the Kingdom of God will find the Whore-(breakout/fully-empowered Antichrist) overcoming and killing the current Kingdom of God (the Christian-Witnesses/Two-Witnesses) at the end of the Sorrows-Period. This will invite the Second Coming of Jesus (who, responds to the attack by initiating a 3.5-year Tribulations-Period-[the Seven Last Plagues of Wrath]).

The second Whore-Movement against the Kingdom of God will find the highly-aggravated Whore (Gog) surrounding the current Kingdom of God (the 144,000 [still mortal, but Christianized] Remnant) on Mt.

Zion, at the end of the Tribulations-Period-(Seven Last Plagues of Wrath). The end-result of this second Whore-Movement will be the complete eradicating of all Whore souls from the face of the Earth (by Jesus and his army of Angels).

The third Whore-Movement against the Kingdom of God will find the Lukewarm populations of the Earth (Magog) finally converting to 'sold-out' Error/Evil— (i.e.; finally agreeing to 'marry' themselves to the Devil, and serve him); at the end of the 1,000-Year-Reign. At that time, they will surround the current Kingdom of God (the 1,000-year-old [immortalized] Remnant) on Mt. Zion, in preparation to destroy them and take back the Earth. In that moment, this last group of ungodly mankind (formerly known as the Lukewarm/Magog) will be instantly devoured by flame, from God.

On the lighter side; when the scripture speaks of the '10th Part', it refers to Kingdom-Seed that will be harvested (and rained back down into the 144,000/Remnant of Israel) during the resurrection of the Christian-Witnesses (to awaken the 144,000, to Jesus). God pre-arranged to harvest this excess of

Kingdom-Seed through the harvest of the Christian-Witnesses, solely for the purpose of having extra to rain back down into the 144,000/Remnant. This is the '10th Part' (whatever else the '10th Part' may imply).

Finally, and most importantly (for unraveling the mystery of the 'Revelation of John'), is that; although the Revelation of John was written as one long scroll (like every other book of the Bible) — nevertheless, it can only be effectually interpreted when the six segments of the scroll are laid side by side (from left to right, from first to last); forming a 'grid' of verses that should be read from top to bottom and from left to right (the way we read a letter, in America). In so doing, we discover that many of the events discussed in the Revelation are revisited across several segments of the scroll (unfolding in exactly the same sequence, as we move down the columns). Each time an event is revisited in the next segment, further details are provided about that event. This is our proof that the grid-layout is correct. — (See; Fig. 3 [pg. 39]) — (Also, see; Appendix A; Revelation Grid Key).

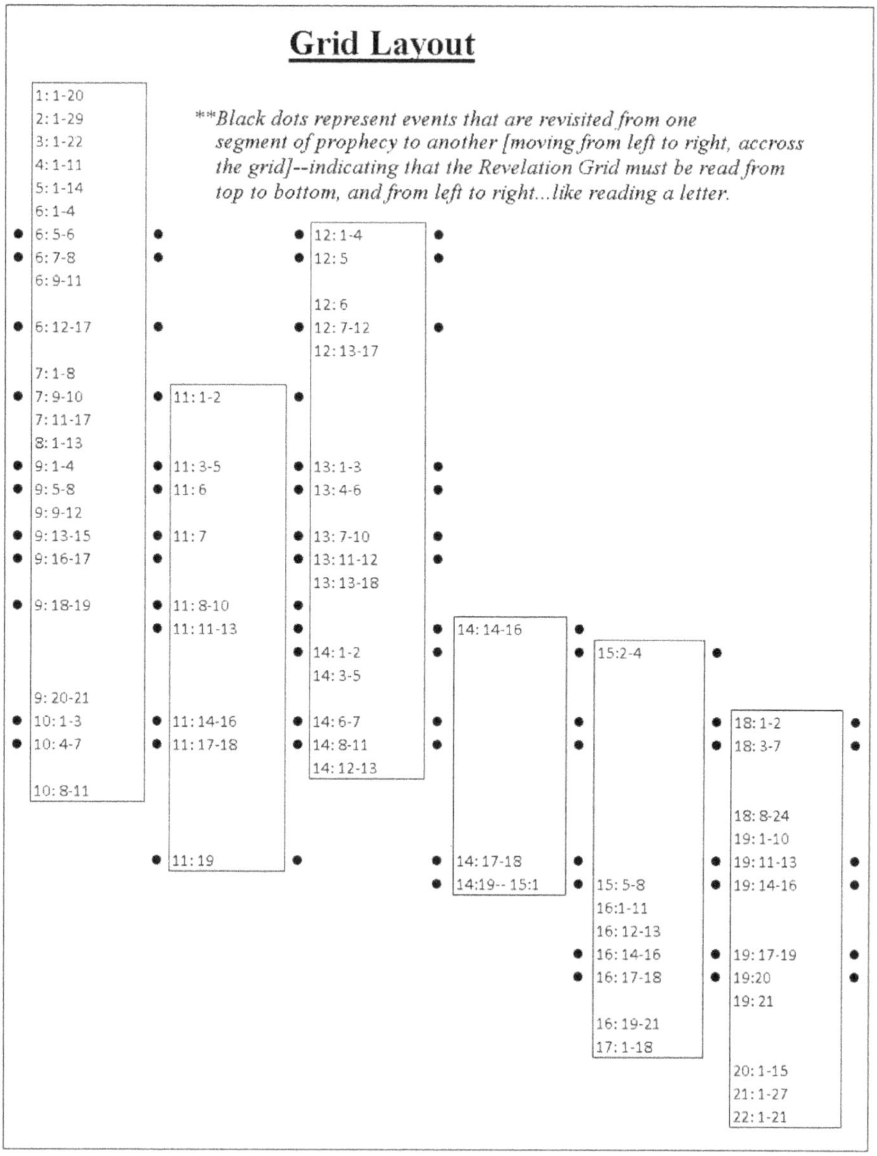
Grid Layout
**Black dots represent events that are revisited from one segment of prophecy to another [moving from left to right, accross the grid]--indicating that the Revelation Grid must be read from top to bottom, and from left to right...like reading a letter.
1:1-20
2:1-29
3:1-22
4:1-11
5:1-14
6:1-4
6:5-6
6:7-8
6:9-11
6:12-17
7:1-8
7:9-10
7:11-17
8:1-13
9:1-4
9:5-8
9:9-12
9:13-15
9:16-17
9:18-19
9:20-21
10:1-3
10:4-7
10:8-11
11:1-2
11:3-5
11:6
11:7
11:8-10
11:11-13
11:14-16
11:17-18
11:19
12:1-4
12:5
12:6
12:7-12
12:13-17
13:1-3
13:4-6
13:7-10
13:11-12
13:13-18
14:1-2
14:3-5
14:6-7
14:8-11
14:12-13
14:14-16
14:17-18
14:19-- 15:1
15:2-4
15:5-8
16:1-11
16:12-13
16:14-16
16:17-18
16:19-21
17:1-18
18:1-2
18:3-7
18:8-24
19:1-10
19:11-13
19:14-16
19:17-19
19:20
19:21
20:1-15
21:1-27
22:1-21

(Fig. 3 -- Grid Layout)

This style of disclosure makes perfect sense if we think about the way most people tell a story. For example: A family member bursts through your front door, and announces; "Oh my gosh! I just saw a wreck!

Everyone is dead!" With everyone now staring at him in horror, he will quickly back up to the beginning and start to fill in more details: "It was a car and a truck. The truck ran a stop sign and hit the car!" As he begins to calm down and catch his breath, he will likely back up again to provide even more detail; such as, describing the occupants of each car and their injuries, the weather conditions that contributed to the accident, etc.... To a child, his announcement might sound like a confusing report of multiple car accidents happening all in a row, but a more mature mind is able to weave the fragmented report together into the single, actual event.

In the following pages, you will find the words of God (KJV) typed in italic, and the words of the Revelation of John (in particular) are typed in bold italic. My own thoughts will appear in ordinary type and my own mid-verse interjections will appear in parentheses. I have applied mid-verse interjections liberally throughout this book because they make shorter (and less confusing) work of explanations that would otherwise require much lengthier wording.

CHAPTER 2 — JOHN'S INTRODUCTION TO THE REVELATION

In the introduction to the 'Revelation of John', the risen (victorious) Jesus appears to the apostle John (the son of Zebedee) shortly after Jesus is raised into Heaven. Here, he identifies himself to John, and proceeds to reveal to John the very specific errors that currently exist in the collective-mindset of redeemable mankind. Jesus begins His Revelation by identifying seven distinct churches (or, 'schools of thought'; mindsets which existed in Jesus' day and will also exist in the end-time), and he provides John with a detailed evaluation of each mindset.

From the perspective of God (according to His risen Son), five of these seven groups of humanity currently have a distorted mindset and are heading for eternal damnation. Therefore, Jesus offers corrective instruction for each, pointing them in the direction of repentance. He tells each church exactly what is wrong with their thinking, and he commands them to process this new information he has given them (to the end that they may come to change their mind-['mindset']; which is called, 'repentance').

Two of the Seven Churches (mindsets) are apparently in right standing with God; existing in an unblemished/obedient state (according to the quantity of 'Word' that they have willingly received, so far). Rather than telling these two churches to repent, Jesus simply offers them a word of encouragement; advising them to stay faithful and brave, even unto death. I believe it will become apparent, as we study the Seven Churches, that the two Churches (mindsets) in 'right' standing before God represent the mindsets of (devout) Judaism and (devout) Christianity (whereas; these are the two churches that embrace one or both halves of God's amendments to mankind). Finally, John is commanded to present these Seven Letters of instruction to the Seven Churches of humanity.

43

And so, we begin our study at **Rev 1:1-8,** which reads:

"(1) ***The Revelation of*** (the risen) ***Jesus Christ, which God gave unto him, to shew unto his servants things which must shortly come to pass; and he sent and signified it by his angel unto his servant John-*** (Son of Zebedee). *(2)* ***Who bare record of the Word of God, and of the testimony of Jesus Christ, and of all things that he saw. (3) Blessed is he that reads, and they that hear the Words of this prophecy, and keep those things which are written therein: for the time is at hand. (4) John to the Seven Churches which are in Asia: Grace be unto you, and peace, from him which is, and which was, and which is to come; and from the seven Spirits which are before his throne;*** *(5)* ***And from Jesus Christ, who is the faithful Witness*** (First and Last Words), ***and the first begotten of the dead, and the prince of the kings of the earth. Unto him that loved us, and washed us from our sins in his own blood, (6) And hath made us kings and priests unto God and his Father; to him be glory and dominion for ever and***

ever. Amen. (7) Behold, he cometh with clouds; and every eye shall see Him, and they also which pierced him: and all kindreds of the earth shall wail because of him. Even so, Amen. (8) I am Alpha and Omega, the beginning and the ending, says the Lord, which is, and which was, and which is to come, the Almighty."

(**Rev 1:9-11** goes on, to say):

"(9) I John, who also am your brother, and companion in tribulation, and in the kingdom and patience of Jesus Christ, was in the isle that is called Patmos, for the Word of God, and for the testimony of Jesus Christ. (10) I was in the spirit on the Lord's day, and heard behind me A great voice, as of a trumpet, (11) Saying, I am Alpha and Omega, the first and the last—(i.e.; the First Word and the Last Word; the Old Testament and the New Testament)*: and, What you see, write in a book, and send it unto the Seven Churches which are in Asia; unto Ephesus, and unto Smyrna, and unto Pergamos, and unto Thyatira, and unto Sardis, and unto Philadelphia, and unto Laodicea."*

(**Rev 1:12-16** goes on, to say):

"*(12) And I turned to see the voice that spake with me. and being turned, I saw seven golden candlesticks; (13) And in the midst of the seven candlesticks one like unto the Son of Man, clothed with a garment down to the foot, and girt about the paps with a golden girdle. (14) His head and his hairs were white like wool, as white as snow; and his eyes were as a flame of fire; (15) And his feet like unto fine brass, as if they burned in a furnace; and his voice as the sound of many waters. (16) And he had in his right hand seven stars: and out of his mouth went a sharp two-edged sword: and his countenance was as the sun shines in his strength.*" — (See; Fig. 4 [pg. 46])

(**Rev 1:17-20** goes on, to say):

"*(17) And when I saw him, I fell at his feet as dead. And he laid his right hand upon me, saying unto me, Fear not; I am the first* (Word) *and the last* (Word). *(18) I am he that lives, and was dead; and, behold, I am alive for evermore amen; and have the keys of Hell and of Death (19) write*

(Fig. 4 -- Jesus, with Stars & Angels)

the things which you have seen—(i.e.; things of the past), **and the things which are**—(i.e.; things happening now), **and the things which shall be**

hereafter—(i.e.; things coming in the future)***;*** ***(20)*** ***The mystery of the seven stars which you saw in my right hand, and the seven golden candlesticks. The seven stars*** (in my hand) ***are the angels of the Seven Churches: and the seven candlesticks which you saw are the Seven Churches*** (seven 'mindsets' of mankind)***."*** — (See; Fig. 4 [pg. 46])

The Seven Churches have been a topic of much controversy, throughout the ages. Many theologians believe the Seven Churches represent seven actual/physical churches that existed in Jesus' day. Many others believe the Seven Churches represent seven eras of time spanning the gap between Jesus' day and present-day. Never-the-less, these theologians will be the first to admit that these theories are merely mankind's best educated guess, thus far. For the purposes of our discussion, I will approach the Seven Churches from the only vantage point that is certain; the (well-defined) distinguishing 'mindset' that each group represents. These mindsets existed in Jesus' day, and will still exist in the end-time. On that premise, let's examine the Seven Letters to the Seven Churches. — (See; Fig. 5 [pg. 49])

The First Church evaluated by Jesus is the church called Ephesus. Just as we will see Him do with each of the other six churches (to follow), Jesus carefully chooses the most relative current examples of this group's distorted mindset, and He proceeds to make His case to them. By the time He is finished, it becomes clear that His bottom-line to this school of thought is that they are more focused on the battle (between good and evil) than they are on loving/saving souls- (i.e.; the 'First Works'); seemingly, finding greater purpose in pointing a finger at the one who is not perfect than in nurturing those who fall short in the race. The job of a Child of God is to replenish the (willful) Earth with the good/loving Spirit of God — not, to focus on condemnation. Jesus tells them, in no uncertain terms; they must change their way of thinking (repent) or they will spend eternity in the Lake of Fire. **Rev 2:1-7** reads:

> "*(1) **Unto the angel of the church of Ephesus write; These things says he that holds the seven stars in his right hand, who walks in the midst**

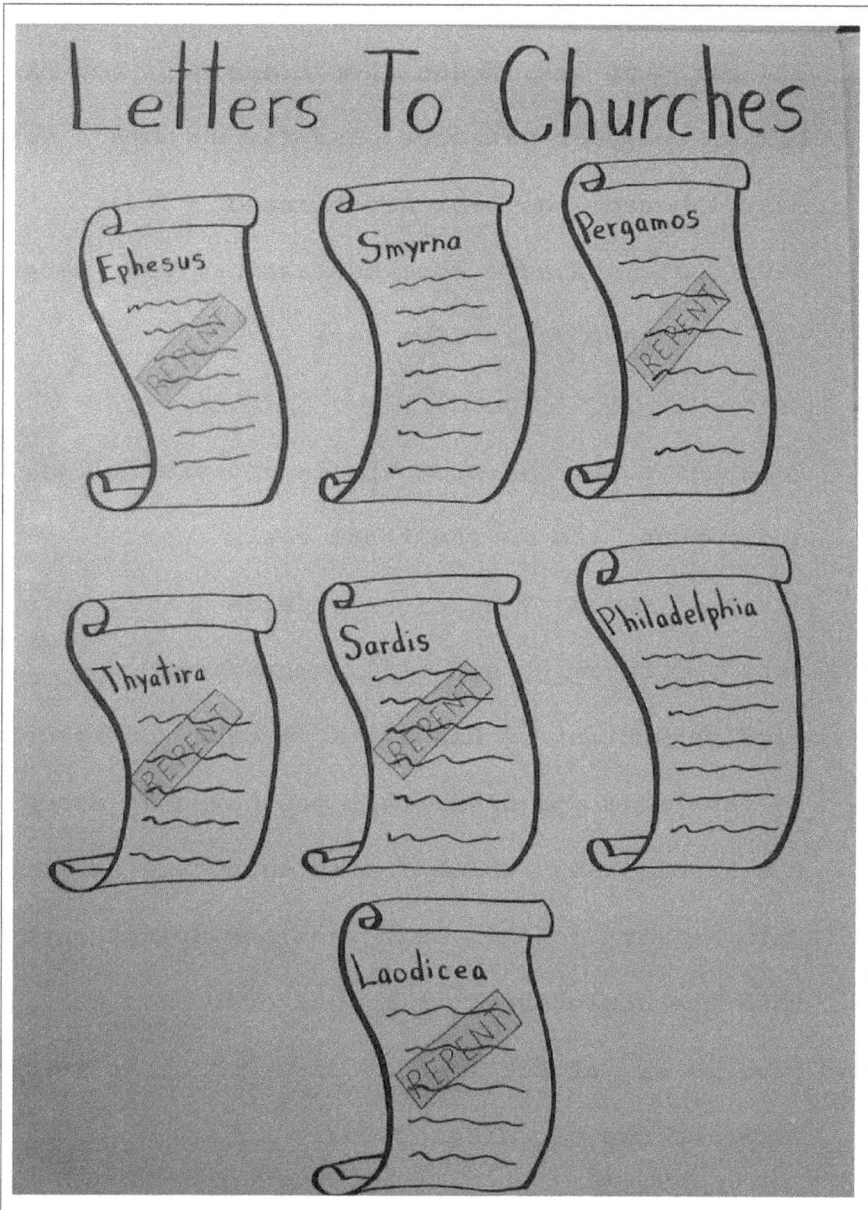

(Fig. 5 -- Letters to Churches)

of the seven golden candlesticks; *(2) I know your*

works, and your labor, and your patience, and how

you canst not bear them which are Evil: and you

have tried them which say they are apostles, and are not, and hast found them liars. (3) And hast borne, and hast patience, and for my name's sake hast labored, and hast not fainted. (4) Nevertheless I have somewhat against you, because you have left your first love (replenishing the Earth with God's good/loving Spirit). *(5) Remember therefore from whence you are fallen, and repent, and do the first works* (producing the fruit of the Holy Spirit)*; or else I will come unto you quickly, and will remove your candlestick out of his place, except you repent. (6) But this you have, that you hate the deeds of the Nicolaitans, which I also hate. (7) He that hath an ear, let him hear what the Spirit says unto the churches; To him that overcomes will I give to eat of the tree of life, which is in the midst of the paradise of God."*

The Second Church evaluated by Jesus is the church called Smyrna. Smyrna is one of the two churches that appear to be in right standing before God (they are not told to repent of anything). I believe Jesus' words of encouragement to this church clearly identifies them as (devout) Jews (the keepers of God's First Word/amendment). His bottom-line to this church-(school of thought) is simply to lean on their faith in Him for the strength to endure all the persecutions they are destined to suffer. **Rev 2:8-11** reads:

> "*(8)* ***And unto the angel of the church in Smyrna write; These things says the first and the last, which was dead, and is alive;*** *(9)* ***I know your works, and tribulation, and poverty, (but you are rich) and I know the blasphemy of them which say they are Jews, and are not***—(i.e.; non-devout Jews), ***but are the synagogue of Satan.*** *(10)* ***Fear none of those things which you shall suffer*** (because of non-devout Jews): ***behold, the Devil shall cast some of you into prison, that ye may be tried; and ye shall have tribulation ten days: Be you faithful unto death, and I will give you a crown of life.*** *(11)* ***He that hath an ear, let him hear what the Spirit says unto the churches; He that overcomes shall not be hurt of the second death***—(i.e.; eternal prison; Lake of Fire)."

The Third Church evaluated by Jesus is the church called Pergamos. Jesus' bottom-line to this church-(school of thought) is that they erroneously attempt to fight the good battle from 'within' Satan's lair (where they are surrounded by Evil). They don't seem to understand that even God himself does not commune with Evil. Nor do they realize that they will be devoured by that Evil (having put themselves into the frying pan). He tells them, in no uncertain terms; they must change their way of thinking (repent) or they will spend eternity in the Lake of Fire. **Rev 2:12-17** reads:

> "*(12)* **And to the angel of the church in Pergamos write; These things says he which hath the sharp sword with two edges;** *(13)* **I know your works, and where you dwell, even where Satan's seat is: and you hold fast my name, and hast not denied my faith, even in those days wherein Antipas was my faithful martyr, who was slain among you, where Satan dwells.** *(14)* **But I have a few things against you, because you have there them that hold the doctrine of Balaam, who taught Balac to cast a stumblingblock before the children of**

Israel, to eat things sacrificed unto idols, and to commit fornication. (15) So hast you also them that hold the doctrine of the Nicolaitans, which thing I hate. (16) Repent; or else I will come unto you quickly, and will fight against them with the sword of my mouth. (17) He that hath an ear, let him hear what the Spirit says unto the churches; To him that overcomes will I give to eat of the hidden manna, and will give him a white stone, and in the stone a new name written, which no man knows saving he that receives it (welcomes it)."

The Fourth Church evaluated by Jesus is the church called Thyatira. Jesus' bottom-line to this church-(school of thought) is that; even though they may not be living within Satan's lair, they erroneously think it harmless to passively tolerate outsiders (sinners) among their own ranks (who, are teaching and practicing idolatry and adultery within hearing-range of their families). They don't seem to understand that permitting this bad example to go unchallenged is giving it the power to seduce and destroy their children. He tells them, in no uncertain terms; they must change their way of thinking (repent) or they will spend eternity in the Lake of Fire. **Rev 2:18-29** reads:

"(18) ***And unto the angel of the church in Thyatira write; These things says the Son of God, who hath his eyes like unto a flame of fire, and his feet are like fine brass;*** *(19)* ***I know your works, and charity, and service, and faith, and your patience, and your works; and the last*** (works) ***to be more than the first*** (works). *(20)* ***Notwithstanding I have a few things against you, because you suffer***-(tolerate) ***that Woman Jezebel, which calls herself a prophetess***—(i.e.; they allow the spirit of her doctrine)***, to teach and to seduce my servants to commit fornication, and to eat things sacrificed unto idols.*** *(21)* ***And I gave her space to repent of her fornication; and she repented not.*** *(22)* ***Behold, I will cast her*** (spirit/doctrine) ***into a bed, and them that commit adultery with her into great tribulation, except they repent of their deeds.*** *(23)* ***And I will kill her children with death; and all the churches shall know that I am he which searches***

the reins and hearts: and I will give unto every one of you according to your works. *(24)* *But unto you I say, and unto the rest in Thyatira, as many as have not this doctrine*—(i.e.; as many as do not approve of tolerating Jezebel's doctrine), *and which have not known the depths of Satan, as they speak*—(i.e.; have not uttered such approval, through their lips); *I will put upon you none other burden.* *(25)* *But that which ye have already hold fast till I come.* *(26)* *And he that overcomes, and keeps my* (first) *works unto the end, to him will I give power over the nations.* *(27)* *And he shall rule them with a rod of iron; as the vessels of a potter shall they be broken to shivers: even as I received of my Father.* *(28)* *And I will give him the morning star.* *(29)* *He that hath an ear, let him hear what the Spirit says unto the churches."*

The Fifth Church evaluated by Jesus is the church called Sardis. Jesus' bottom-line to this church-(school of thought) is that; even though they have managed to attain salvation through Jesus—(i.e.; managed to receive the free gift) they are not yet paying-it-forward (performing Jesus' work upon the earth [such as; loving/forgiving/saving/etc...]; the 'First Works'). They don't seem to understand that they have been saved in order to 'serve God' (the same way that Jesus did; replenishing the [willful] Earth with the Goodness/love of God — the same way that Adam & Eve were supposed to, from the beginning). He tells them, in no uncertain terms; they must change their way of thinking (repent) or they will spend eternity in the Lake of Fire. **Rev 3:1-6** reads:

> "*(1) **And unto the angel of the church in Sardis write; These things says he that hath the seven Spirits of God, and the seven stars; I know your works, that you have a name that you live**—*(i.e.; you've been 'saved')*, **and** (yet) **are dead**—*(i.e.; observed by God to be a dead/unfruitful branch).*
>
> (2) **Be watchful, and strengthen the things which remain, that are ready to die: for I have not found your works perfect before God.** (3) **Remember therefore how you have received and heard, and hold fast, and repent. If therefore you shall not watch, I will come on you as a thief, and you shall not know what hour I will come upon you.**

(4) you have a few names even in Sardis which have not defiled their garments; and they shall walk with me in white: for they are worthy. (5) He that overcomes, the same shall be clothed in white raiment; and I will not blot out his name out of the book of life, but I will confess his name before my Father, and before his angels. (6) He that hath an ear, let him hear what the Spirit says unto the churches."

The Sixth Church evaluated by Jesus is the church called Philadelphia. This is the second of the two churches that appear to be in right standing before God; they are not told to repent of anything. I believe Jesus' words of encouragement to this church clearly identifies them as the Christian-Witnesses (the faithful keepers of both the First and Last 'Words'). His bottom-line to this church-(school of thought) is simply to hold fast to their free gift (salvation), proclaim Christ's Word to the world, and be patient and faithful unto death. Rev **3:7-13** reads:

"(7) And to the angel of the church in Philadelphia write; These things says he that is holy, he that is true, he that hath the key of

David, he that opens, and no man shuts; and shuts, and no man opens—(i.e.; the doors of Heaven); *(8) I know your works: behold, I have set before you an open door, and no man can shut it: for you have a little strength, and hast kept my Word, and hast not denied my name*—('Savior'; performing First Works). *(9) Behold, I will make them of the synagogue of Satan, which say they are Jews, and are not, but do lie*—(i.e.; non-devout Jews); *behold, I will make them to come and worship before your feet, and to know that I have loved you. (10) Because you have kept the Word of my patience, I also will keep you from the hour of temptation* (Tribulations-Period), *which shall come upon all the world, to try them that dwell upon the earth. (11) Behold; I come quickly: hold that fast which you have, that no man take your crown. (12) Him that overcomes will I make a pillar in the temple of my God, and he shall go no more out: and I will write upon him the name of my God, and the name of the city of my God, which is new Jerusalem, which cometh down out of heaven from my God: and I will write upon* *him my new name. (13) **He that hath an ear, let him hear what the Spirit says unto the churches.**"*

The Seventh Church evaluated by Jesus is the church called Laodicea. Jesus' bottom-line to this church-(school of thought) is that they arrogantly worship only 'self'; disregarding any need to bring self-will under allegiance to anyone else's will; either God or the Devil. They don't seem to understand that by refusing to follow God's lead, they leave themselves unwitting puppets of the Devil, by default. He tells them, in no uncertain terms; they must change their way of thinking (repent) or they will spend eternity in the Lake of Fire. **Rev 3:14-22** reads:

"*(14)* **And unto the angel of the church of the Laodiceans write; These things says the Amen, the faithful and true Witness, the beginning of the creation of God;** *(15)* **I know your works, that you are neither cold nor hot**—(i.e.; have not yet made your free-will decision between God and Devil)**:** **I would you wert cold or hot.** *(16)* **So then because you are lukewarm, and neither cold nor hot, I will spew you out of my mouth.** *(17)* **Because you say, I am rich, and increased with goods, and** *have need of nothing*—(i.e.; I don't need God; I can take care of myself)*; and know not that you are wretched, and miserable, and poor, and blind, and naked.* (18) *I counsel you to buy of me gold tried in the fire, that you may be rich; and white raiment, that you may be clothed, and that the shame of your nakedness do not appear; and anoint thine eyes with eyesalve, that you may see* (the Truth). (19) *As many as I love, I rebuke and chasten: be zealous therefore, and repent.* (20) *Behold, I stand at the door, and knock: if any man hear my voice, and open the door, I will come in to him, and will sup with him, and he with me.* (21) *To him that overcomes will I grant to sit with me in my throne, even as I also overcame, and am set down with my Father in his throne.* (22) *He that hath an ear, let him hear what the Spirit says unto the churches.*"

CHAPTER 3 — VISION OF JESUS AND THE BOOK OF SEVEN SEALS

Once the risen Jesus has clearly described the (redeemable) errors that exist within humanity — and, the proposed cures for them — he moves on to provide a series of visions that detail the entire crisis at issue before the throne of God (which threatens all of creation), and the means by which Jesus came to be given full authority to resolve that crisis. **Rev 4:1-11** reads:

> "*(1) After this I looked, and, behold, a door was opened in heaven: and the first voice which I heard was as it were of a trumpet talking with me; which said, Come up hither, and I will shew you things which must be hereafter*—(i.e.; in the future). *(2) And immediately I was in the spirit:*

and, behold, a throne was set in heaven, and one sat on the throne. *(3)* *And he that sat was to look upon like a jasper and a sardine stone: and there was a rainbow around the throne, in sight like unto an emerald.* *(4)* *And round about the throne were four and twenty seats: and upon the seats I saw four and twenty elders sitting* (12 Early Saints & 12 apostles)*, clothed in white raiment; and they had on their heads crowns of gold.* *(5)* *And out of the throne proceded lightnings and thunderings and voices: and there were seven lamps of fire burning before the throne, which are the seven spirits of God*—(i.e.; the seven angels of the Seven Churches, standing before God). *(6)* *And before the throne there was a Sea of Glass like unto crystal: and in the midst of the throne, and round about the throne, were four Beasts full of eyes before and behind.* *(7)* *And the first Beast was like a lion* (wild animal)*, and the second Beast like a calf* (domesticated animal)*, and the third Beast had a face as a man* (mankind)*, and the fourth Beast was like a flying eagle* (fowl). *(8)* *And the four*

Beasts had each of them six wings about him; and they were full of eyes within: and they rest not day and night, saying, Holy, holy, holy, Lord God Almighty, which was, and is, and is to come. (9) And when those Beasts give glory and honor and thanks to him that sat on the throne, who lives for ever and ever, (10) The four and twenty elders fall down before him that sat on the throne, and worship him that lives for ever and ever, and cast their crowns before the throne, saying, (11) you are worthy, O Lord-(God)*, to receive glory and honor and power: for you have created all things, and for your pleasure they are and were created."* — (See; Fig. 6 [pg. 64])

(**Rev 5:1-5** goes on, to say):

"(1) And I saw in the right hand of him-(God) *that sat on the throne a book* (of Seven Seals) *written within and on the backside, sealed with seven seals. (2) And I saw a strong angel proclaiming with a loud voice, Who is worthy to open the book, and to loose the seals thereof? (3) And no man in heaven* (realm of light)*, nor in*

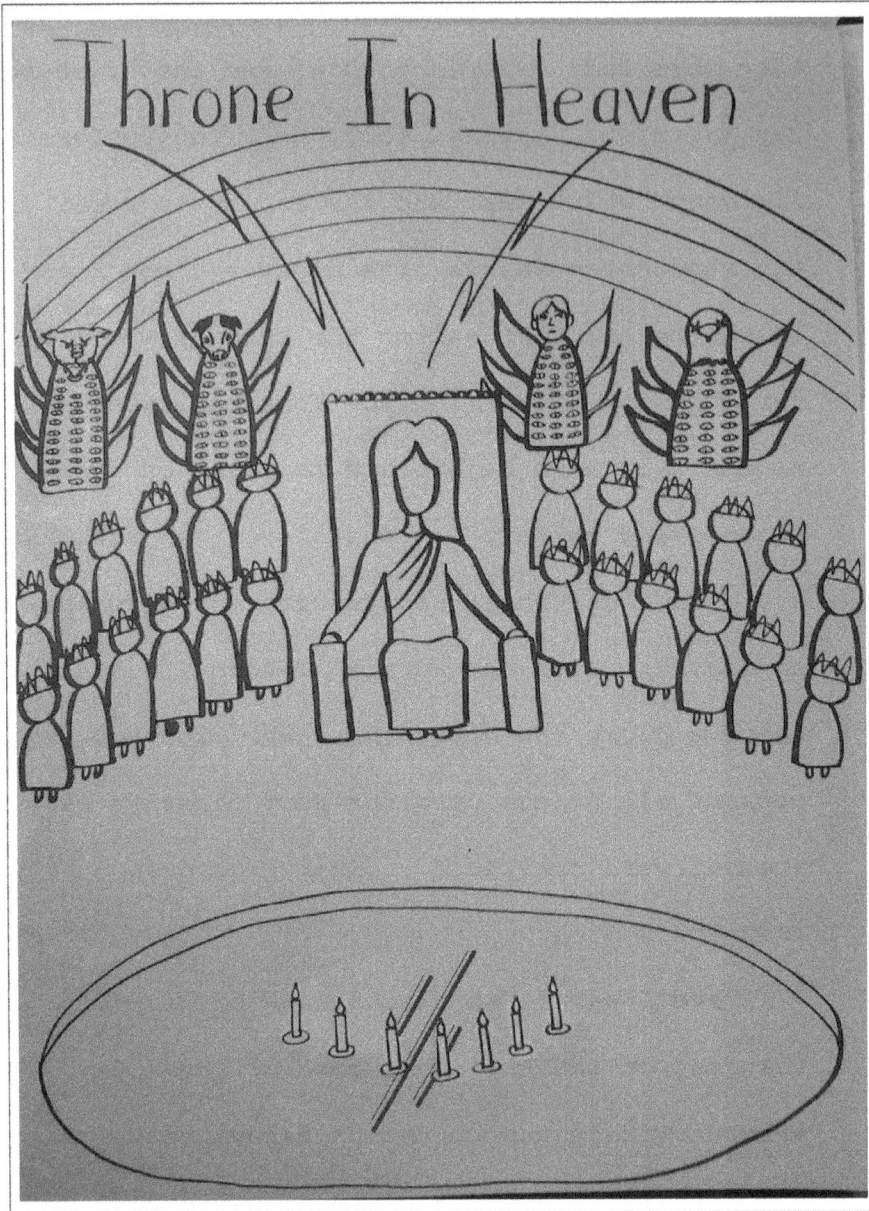

(Fig. 6 -- Throne Room)

earth (realm of man)**, neither under the earth**
(realm of darkness)**, was able to open the book,**
neither to look thereon. *(4) And I wept much,*

because no man was found worthy to open and to read the book, neither to look thereon. *(5)* **And one of the elders says unto me, Weep not: behold, the Lion of the tribe of Juda, the Root of David** (Jesus) **hath prevailed to open the book, and to loose the Seven Seals thereof."** — (See; Fig. 7 [pg. 66])

In the verses that follow, we'll see that the willing death of Jesus (the innocent Lamb of God) is made to fulfill the death sentence that was imposed upon all of mankind (in the Garden of Eden). And we see that Jesus' willing sacrifice for mankind is what earned him complete authority and power over all of creation. **Rev 5:6-14** goes on, to say:

"(6) **And I beheld, and, lo, in the midst of the throne and of the four Beasts, and in the midst of the elders, stood a lamb as it had been slain** (the crucified/risen Jesus)**, having seven horns and seven eyes, which are the seven spirits of god sent forth into all the earth**—(i.e.; the Seven Angels [of the Seven Churches] are a part of the 'head' of Christ)*. (7)* **And he-**(the Lamb) **came and took the book out of the right hand of**

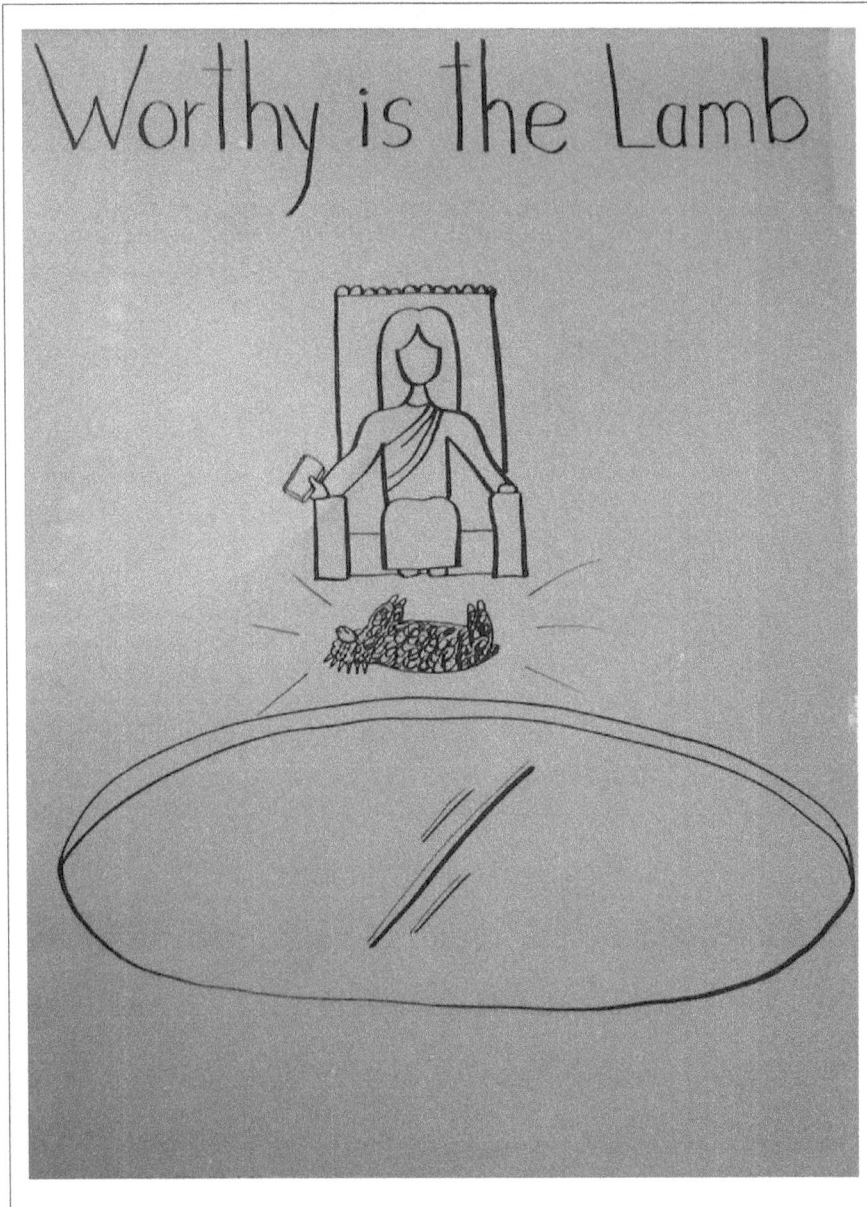

(Fig. 7 -- Slain Lamb of God)

him-(God) *that sat upon the throne. (8) And when*
he had taken the book, the four Beasts and four
and twenty elders fell down before the Lamb,

having every one of them harps, and golden vials full of odors, which are the prayers of saints. *(9)* **And they sung a new song, saying, Thou-**(Jesus) **are worthy to take the book, and to open the seals thereof: for you were slain, and hast redeemed us**-(the 4 beasts and 24 elders) **to God by your blood out of every kindred, and tongue, and people, and nation;** *(10)* **And hast made us unto our God kings and priests: and we shall reign on the earth.** *(11)* **And I beheld, and I heard the voice of many angels round about the throne and the Beasts and the elders: and the number of them**-(the angels) **was ten thousand times ten thousand, and thousands of thousands;** *(12)* **Saying with a loud voice, Worthy is the Lamb that was slain to receive power, and riches, and wisdom, and strength, and honor, and glory, and blessing.** *(13)* **And every creature which is in heaven, and on the earth, and under the earth, and such as are in the sea, and all that are in them, heard I saying, Blessing, and honor, and glory, and power, be unto him that sits upon the throne, and unto the Lamb for ever and ever.** *(14)*

And the four Beasts said, Amen. And the four and twenty elders fell down and worshipped him that lives for ever and ever."

And now we come to the heart of the 'Revelation of John'; the systematic disclosure of the events which lie behind the Seven Seals. So important to mankind is the understanding of this disclosure, that God tells us at the beginning of the book (Rev 1:3); *"Blessed is he that reads, and they that hear the Words of this prophecy, and keep those things which are written therein: for the time is at hand."* And at the end of the book (Rev 22:7), he repeats again; *"Blessed is he that keeps the sayings of the prophecy of this book."* These statements represent a double-blessing to every soul who is determined to meditate on the 'Revelation of John'. With that blessing in mind, we'll follow along with Jesus as he unfolds the mystery of the Seven Seals.

When the risen Jesus breaks open the First Seal, a vision reveals the short-story of a powerful character that had a defined purpose in the history of mankind. If we look closely, this story mirrors the role that Adam plays, in the history and destiny of mankind. **Rev 6:1-2** reads:

> *"(1) **And I saw when the Lamb opened one of the seals, and I heard, as it were the noise of thunder, one of the four Beasts saying, Come and see.** (2) **And I saw, and behold a white horse: and he that sat on him had a bow; and a crown was given unto him: and he went forth conquering, and to conquer.**"* — (See; Fig. 8 [pg. 70])

As we see over and over again in the Bible; when Prophecy depicts an entity riding on an animal (a horse, in this case), the animal represents the 'power' behind the rider. The above story is reminiscent of how Adam-(mankind) first appeared on the scene, with power, and was supposed to rule over the Earth; to fill/replenish the (willful) Earth with the Goodness/love of God (our 'boss', by original design) so that good-will (rather than free-will) would rule over the entire creation. Consider the following verse from the book of Genesis, in which Adam mirrors the story of the First Horseman:

> *(Ref: Gen 1:28)—"And God said to them-(Adam/Eve), Be fruitful...and replenish the earth...subdue*

(Fig. 8 -- Four Horsemen)

it...have dominion over...every living thing that moves upon the earth."

Similarly; when the risen Jesus breaks open the Second Seal, the book reveals another short-story of a powerful character that had a defined purpose in the history of mankind. If we look closely, this story mirrors the role that the Serpent (or, Devil) plays, in the history and destiny of mankind. **Rev 6:3-4** reads:

> "*(3)* ***And when he had opened the second seal, I heard the second Beast say, Come and see.*** *(4)* ***And there went out another horse that was red: and power was given to him that sat thereon to take peace*** (away) ***from the earth, and that they should kill one another***—(i.e.; Adam -vs.- Serpent; Good -vs.- Evil)*: **and there was given unto him*** (Devil) ***a great sword*** (weapon of death/destruction).*" —* (See; Fig. 8 [pg. 70])

This story is reminiscent of how the Devil appeared before Adam & Eve in the Garden, focusing all his energy on destroying the 'good' that God's man was supposed to accomplish on Earth. Consider the following verse from the book of Genesis, which mirrors the dynamic at work between the first two horsemen:

(Ref: Gen 3:15)—"And I-(God) *will put enmity between you-*(Devil) *and the Woman-*(collective-soul of mankind)*...it-*(mankind) *shall bruise your head* (your 'mindset' of *Error/Evil) and you-* (Devil) *shall bruise his heel* (his 'walk'/progress)."

When the risen Jesus breaks open the Third Seal, the book reveals another short-story of a powerful character that had a defined purpose in the history of mankind. If we look closely, this story mirrors the role that Israel plays in the history and destiny of mankind (having received the First Word/Witness of God). **Rev 6:5-6** reads:

"(5) **And when he had opened the third seal, I heard the third Beast say, Come and see. And I beheld, and lo a black horse; and he that sat on him had a pair of balances** (the scales of justice) **in his hand.** *(6)* **And I heard a voice in the midst of the four Beasts say, A measure of wheat for a penny, and three measures of barley for a penny**—(i.e.; same price for everything)*;* **and see you hurt not the oil & the wine** (the anointed of God)." — (See; Fig. 8 [pg. 70])

This story is reminiscent of when God sent the spirit of Law & Prophecy (the First Word/amendment) into the world, through Israel; which uncovered sin, and simultaneously defined just punishment for it (as well as providing a promise of atonement, from it; one price for all sin). God steeped Israel in the Word/knowledge of discerning right from wrong (via Old Testament Law) so they could begin to judge among themselves justly (so that God's anointed would not be harmed, unjustly). Consider the following verse from the book of Isaiah which mirrors this rich awakening and anointing on Israel, and tells us exactly what God expected back from Israel, in return for that gift:

> (Ref: Isa 5:7)—*"For the vineyard of the Lord of hosts is the house of Israel, and the men of Judah his pleasant plant: and he looked for* (good) *judgment* (from them), *but behold* (they produced) *oppression;* (He looked) *for righteousness* (from them), *but behold a cry* (of injustice)."

If we move across the Revelation Grid (from left to right)—(See; Fig. 3 [pg. 39]), we find that Chapter

12 revisits Israel's rise and fall, adding further detail to this 3rd seal scenario. **Rev 12:1-4** reads:

> "*(1)* **And there appeared a great wonder in heaven;** **a Woman** (collective-soul of mankind) **clothed with the sun, and the moon under her feet, and upon her head a crown of twelve stars** (the twelve tribes of Israel; full of anointed life-force energy/power). *(2)* **And she**-(the Woman) **being** (pregnant) **with child** (the Messiah) **cried, travailing in birth, and pained to be delivered.** *(3)* **And there appeared another wonder in heaven; and behold a great red Dragon**-(the Devil), **having seven heads and ten horns, and seven crowns upon his heads.** *(4)* **And his tail drew the third part of the stars of heaven** (Israel; the anointed Witnesses of God-[the 3rd Part]), **and did cast them to the earth**—(i.e.; Devil seduced them and led them to their fall): **and the Dragon stood before the Woman**-(collective-soul of mankind) **which was ready to be delivered, for to devour her child** (the Messiah) **as soon as it was born.**"
> — (See; Fig. 8 [pg. 70])

In verse 4, above, we see the first appearance of the words '3rd Part' and how they apply to the text of this 3rd Seal event. Understanding that the 3rd Part refers to vessels (or, 'bodies') possessing the anointed life-force energy/power of God (and that during this period of history, the children of Israel were the only 'human' vessels in that category) we can begin to make the connection between the event details discussed in Rev 6 & Rev 12 (which both speak of the 3rd Part). Consider the following verse from the book of Deuteronomy, in which the words '3rd generation' (or, 'part') are applied to some gentiles who will become converted to Christianity in the distant future (bringing them into the ranks of anointed children of God [or, '3rd Part']):

> *(Ref: Deu 23:8)*—"*The children*-(descendants) *that are begotten of them*-(the Edomites and Egyptians-[Gentiles]) *shall enter into the congregation of the Lord* (anointed status) *in their third generation*—(i.e.; when they become Christianized; reborn as 3rd Part)."

When the risen Jesus breaks open the Fourth Seal, the book reveals yet another short-story of a powerful character that had a defined purpose in the history of mankind. If we look closely, this story mirrors the role that Jesus plays, in the history and destiny of mankind. **Rev 6:7-8** reads:

> "*(7) **And when he had opened the fourth seal, I heard the voice of the fourth Beast say, Come and see.** (8) **And I looked, and behold a pale horse; and his name that sat on him was Death**—(i.e.; He was marked for death, from the moment he appeared on the scene)**, and Hell-**(the grave) **followed with him. And power** (authority) **was given unto them** (the rider and the grave) **over the fourth part of the earth**—(i.e.; over the destruction of the flesh, during the reign of the Fourth Kingdom [4ᵗʰ Part])**; to kill with sword, and with hunger, and with death, and with the Beasts of the earth** (See; Rev 1:18)." — (See; Fig. 8 [pg. 70])*

This story is reminiscent of the way Jesus Christ came into the world with a death-sentence on his head, and Hell-(the grave) thought to swallow him up. But, through the power of Jesus' willing blood-letting (death and resurrection), he overpowered death and the grave. God rewarded Jesus by giving him full charge

over the final destruction of 'all things physical'
(beginning at the Fourth Kingdom [4th Part]), and Hell-
(the grave) was guaranteed her spoils. It makes sense
to me that this horse was pale as a symbolic reference
to the 'blood-letting' of Jesus. Consider the
following verses, which should help make the
connection between Jesus and the above verse even more
apparent:

(Ref: Heb 2:14-15)—"(14) Forasmuch then as the
children (of the Kingdom of God) *are partakers of*
flesh and blood, he-(Jesus) *also himself likewise*
took part of the same—(i.e.; He took part of a
physical body)*; that through death he might*
destroy him that had the power of death, that is,
the Devil; (15) And deliver them-(mankind) *who*
through fear of death were all their lifetime
subject to bondage."

And...

(Ref: Luke 18:31-33)—"(31) Then he-(Jesus)...*said*
unto them, Behold, we go up to Jerusalem, and all
things that are written by the prophets
concerning the Son of man-(me) *shall be*
accomplished. (32) For he-(Son of Man) *shall be*

delivered unto the Gentiles, and shall be mocked,

and spitefully entreated, and spitted on: (33)

And they shall scourge him, and put him to death:

and the third day he shall rise again."

These verses reflect that Jesus was born into the world for the express purpose of being killed (to pay the debt of all mankind) — and, that being completely aware of the horror of his own earthly end, Jesus still made that sacrifice willingly.

It is here, at the 4th Seal prophecy (Rev 6:7-8, above) that we find the first appearance of the words '4th Part', and begin to get a sense of their meaning. The following verses are intended to support the presupposition that the words '4th Part' represent the Fourth Kingdom on Earth; the Whore-souls of the Whore-Movements (against the Kingdom of God):

(Ref: Gen 15:16)—"But in the fourth generation—
(i.e.; during the Whore-Movements of Antichrist) *they-*(the children of Israel) *shall come hither again* (be gathered together again, at Jerusalem)*: for the iniquity of the Amorites is not yet full."*

And...

(Ref: Numb 23:10)—"Who can count the dust of Jacob (the physical bodies of Israel), *and the number of the fourth part of Israel* (the number of Israel who will be counted part of the Whore/Whore-Movements)*?"*

And...

(Ref: II King 10:30)—"And the Lord said unto Jehu-(a Jew), *Because you have done well in executing that which is right in mine eyes, and hast done unto the house of Ahab according to all that was in mine heart, your children of the fourth generation—*(i.e.; his [Jewish] descendants, alive during the Whore-Movements) *shall* (be redeemed, to) *sit on the throne of Israel—*(i.e.; Jehu's descendants [Jews] will be plucked out from the Whore-Movements-[4th Part] to enter back into the ranks of the Kingdom of God [3rd Part]; this verse is a reference to that portion of the 144,000/Remnant which will be descended from Jehu's own lineage)."

And...

(Ref: Numb 14:18 [& Exo 34:7])—"The Lord is longsuffering, and of great mercy, forgiving

iniquity and transgression, and by no means clearing the guilty (without punishment), *visiting the iniquity* (guilt) *of the fathers upon the children unto the third and fourth generation*—(i.e.; unto the 144,000/Remnant [3rd-Part] as well as unto the ungodly [4th-Part], in the Tribulations-Period.) "

If we move across the Revelation Grid (from left to right)—(See; Fig. 3 [pg. 39]), we find that Chapter 12 revisits the birth/death/resurrection of Jesus and his reward [of power and authority, at God's side] for that victory). **Rev 12:5** reads:

"*(5)* **And she**-(Israel; 'prepared'-mankind) **brought forth a man child**-(Jesus)**, who was to rule all nations with a rod of iron** (the Messiah)**: and her child was caught up unto God, and to his throne**—(i.e.; Jesus was born, was raised, was killed, was glorified, and ascended to the right hand of God)." — (See; Fig. 8 [pg. 70])

When the risen Jesus breaks open the Fifth Seal, the book reveals another short-story; this one, introducing us to a group of resurrected souls who suddenly appeared under the alter of God (on the Sea of Glass) when the resurrected Jesus' ascended into Heaven (Matt 27:52). **Rev 6:9-11** reads:

> "*(9) And when he had opened the fifth seal, I saw under the altar the souls of them* (many of the Saints of Israel) *that were slain for the Word of God, and for the testimony which they held*—(i.e.; they who possessed the First Witness [within], and also believed the prophecy of the second Witness [yet to come]; these had died, openly professing their faith in both Witnesses). *(10) And they cried with a loud voice, saying, How long, O Lord, holy and true, dost you not judge and avenge our blood* (martyrs) *on them that dwell on the earth? (11) And white robes were given unto every one of them; and it was said unto them, that they should rest yet for a little season, until their fellow-servants also and their brethren, that should be killed as they were*—(i.e.; for Jesus' name's sake), *should be fulfilled*—(i.e.; they should rest on the Sea of Glass, until the last two harvests are also completed)." — (See; Fig. 9 [pg. 82])

(Fig. 9 -- Souls Under Altar)

If we look closely, this story mirrors the role of the 'many saints' who were resurrected at the time of Jesus' resurrection (mentioned in Matt 27:52). This first harvest (the 'Early-Saints' of Israel) were raised from their graves, walked the Earth, and were raised to the Sea of Glass-(under the altar of God) during Jesus' ascension; where they would then have to wait for the rest of redeemable mankind to join them (in the end-time)—(See; Fig. 10[a] [pg. 84]). Consider the following verses from the book of Matthew, which detail this earliest time of harvest:

> *(Ref: Math 27:50-53)—"(50) Jesus, when he had cried again with a loud voice* (while being crucified)*, yielded up the ghost* (dying)*....And the graves were opened; and many bodies of the saints which slept-*(dead/buried) *arose, (53) And came out of the graves after his-*(Jesus') *resurrection..."*

Even from the foundation of the world, God's harvest schedule has been set for 'a time', 'times' and 'a dividing of a time'. This Fifth Seal depicts the harvest of these Early-Saints (the first 'time'). As we will see later; the Sixth Trump will depict the harvest of the Christian-Witnesses/Two-Witnesses ('times'), and the Seventh Trump will depict the harvest of the 144,000/Remnant of Israel (the

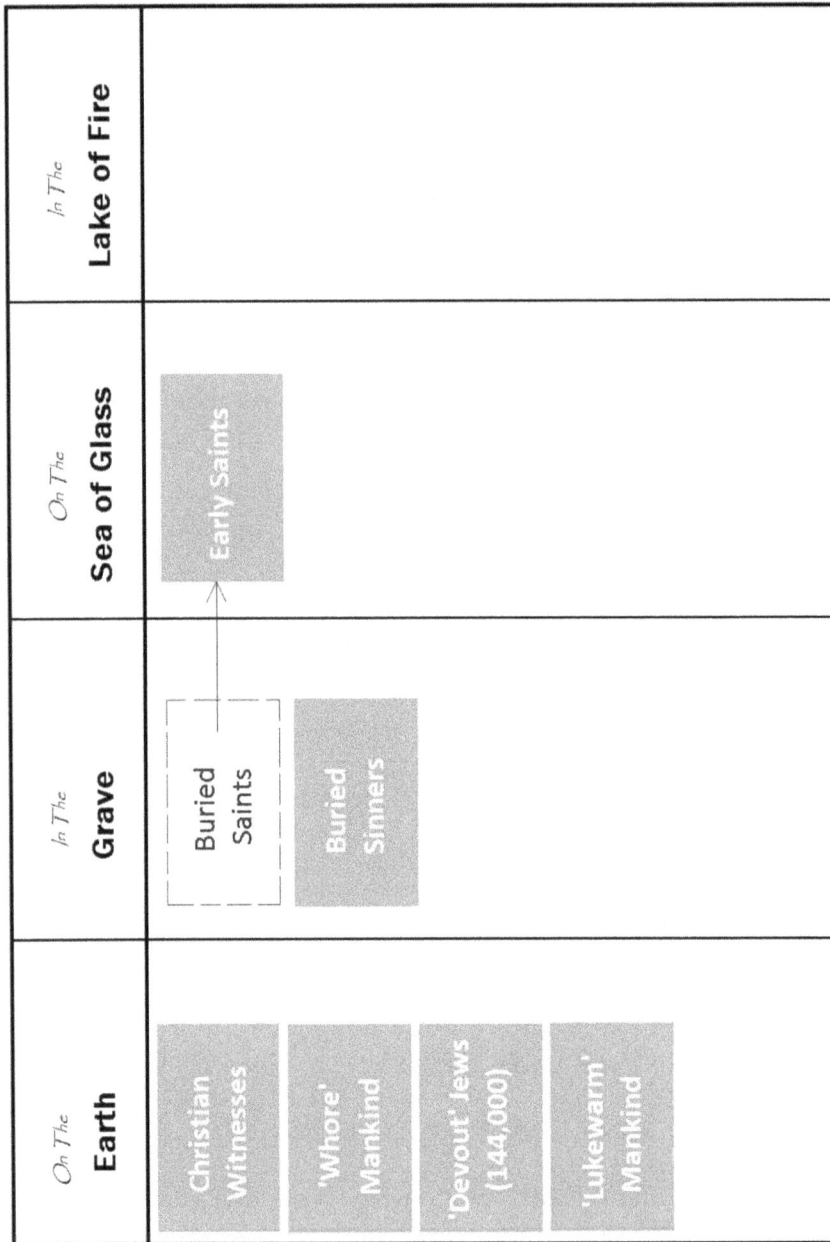

(Fig. 10a – Early Saints Harvested to Sea of Glass)

'dividing of time' [the fractional/remnant harvest]).

Moving down the Revelation Grid; Chapter 12 goes

on to tell us that immediately after Jesus' victory

over death, Israel was scattered among the wilderness

of ungodly mankind, with Judaism-(the 'First-Amendment-only' religion) blinded to Jesus-(the Last-Word/amendment) until the end-time, when a devout Remnant of Israel will be awakened to Jesus, and saved. **Rev 12:6** reads:

> "*(6)* ***And the Woman***-(Collective-soul of 'prepared'-mankind) ***fled into the wilderness***-(the place of ungodliness)***, where she hath a place prepared of God*** (a designated period of time)***, that they***-(God's ministers) ***should feed her there*** (ministering to her)***...a thousand two hundred and threescore days*** (3.5 years)." — (See; Fig. 9 [pg. 82])

Even though God had temporarily 'sealed' the door on Judaism-(the 'First-Amendment-only' religion) in His anger — and scattered the people of Israel throughout all the world (due to the blasphemy [of her rulers] against the Holy Spirit of Truth) — still, God would not abandon the 'people' of Israel (the Lost Sheep). Not only would He (eventually) provide the above mentioned eleventh-hour means of escape for the 144,000—(i.e.; the end-time 'grace'), but all the descendants of Israel's bloodlines (each individual soul) would also have centuries of opportunity to escape (at any time) between the time of Jesus' resurrection and the Sorrows/Tribulations-Period — simply by becoming willing to hear the Gospel of the New Testament (through which, the Holy Spirit promises to open their eyes to Jesus/Truth). Consider the following verses that attest to God's patient love toward the Lost-Sheep of Israel:

> *(Ref: II Chron 21:7)—" Howbeit the Lord would not destroy the house of David, because of the covenant that he had made with David, and as he promised to give a light to him and to his sons for ever."*

And...

> *(Ref: Deu 4:27-31)—"(27) The lord shall scatter you-*(Israel) *among the nations, and ye shall be left few in number among the heathen, whither the Lord shall lead you. (28) And there ye shall serve gods, the work of men's hands, wood and stone, which neither see, nor hear, nor eat, nor smell. (29) But if from thence* (from the wilderness) *you shall seek the Lord your God* (earnestly seek Truth), *you shall find him, if*

you seek him with all your heart and with all your soul—(i.e.; if you keep the Old Testament, and truly seek God/Truth, you will be led to the New Testament...and there, the Holy Spirit will finish your amendment and you will be saved).

(30) When you are in tribulation, and all these things are come upon you, even in the latter days (even in the end-times), *if you turn to the Lord your God, and shall be obedient unto his voice* (drawing you to Jesus); *(31) (For the Lord your God is a merciful God;) he will not forsake you, neither destroy you, nor forget the covenant of your fathers which he swore unto them."*

And...

(Ref: Jer 31:31-34)—"(31) Behold....I will make a new covenant with the house of Israel—(i.e.; the New Testament Covenant), *and with the house of Judah: (32) Not according to the covenant that I made with their fathers* (the Old Testament covenant)...*which my covenant they broke, although I was an* (good/true) *husband unto them....But this shall be the covenant that I will make with the house of Israel; after those*

days (end-times; after the harvest of the
Christian-Witnesses), *says the Lord, I will put
my law in their inward parts* (awakening the
144,000/Remnant), *and write it in their hearts;
and will be their God, and they shall be my
people. (34) And they shall teach no more every
man his neighbor, and every man his brother,
saying, Know the Lord—*(i.e.; won't be
evangelizing each other): *for they shall all know
me* (at once), *from the least of them unto the
greatest of them, says the Lord: for I will
forgive their iniquity, and I will remember their
sin no more* (144,000 of them)."

And...

*(Ref: II King 19:31)—"For out of Jerusalem shall
go forth a Remnant-*(the 144,000), *and they that
escape out of mount Zion: the zeal of the Lord of
hosts shall do this."*

As we see in Jer 31:31-34, above, God states that
Israel broke His covenant with them (Old Testament
covenant), but He explains that He will save them in
the end-time under the 'New' covenant (New Testament
covenant; through Jesus).

Returning to the Revelation; when the risen Jesus breaks open the Sixth Seal, the book reveals another short-story; this one, describing violent events taking place in Heaven and on Earth (immediately after Jesus' resurrection); stars falling to Earth and Heaven being sealed up—(See; Fig. 11 [pg. 90]). **Rev 6:12-17** reads:

*"(12) **And I beheld when he had opened the sixth seal, and, lo, there was a great earthquake; and the sun became black as sackcloth of hair, and the moon became as blood; (13) And the stars of Heaven fell unto the earth**—(i.e.; Satan & his Legion of angels were eternally banished to Earth at the time of Jesus' victory; with all access to the throne of God [Heaven] cut off, for eternity), **even as a fig tree casts her untimely** (incomplete) **figs, when she is shaken of a mighty wind. (14) And the Heaven departed as a scroll when it is rolled together**—(i.e.; God's amending Word/council was closed to Satan and his Legion; forever closed, like a book); **and every mountain and island** (on earth) **were moved out of their places. (15) And the kings of the earth, and the***

(Fig. 11 -- Devil Cast Out of Heaven)

great men, and the rich men, and the chief

captains, and the mighty men, and every bondman,

and every free man, hid themselves in the dens

and in the rocks of the mountains; (16) And said to the mountains and rocks, fall on us, and hide us from the face of him that sits on the throne, and from the wrath of the (glorified) *Lamb. (17) For the great day of His wrath is come; and who shall be able to stand?"*

If we look closely, this story mirrors the one-sided battle that took place immediately after Jesus' resurrection (this will be better illustrated by upcoming passages). This is a powerful glimpse into what took place on Earth and in Heaven when Michael (an archangel-representation of the Lord) received full authority to take hold of the Serpent (and his dark angels) and cast them down into their earthly prison; sealing them off from Heaven (and from God's amending Word), for eternity. Prior to Jesus' victory-(crucifixion and resurrection), Satan had been able to appear before God whenever he wanted (along with all the other angels, dark and light). But after the victorious Jesus' cast them into their earthly prison, they could no longer appear before God's throne. Jesus sealed the fate of the Devil and his Legions in a way that mankind could now be eternally separated from them.

Consider the following verses, which rehearse the unlimited access Satan used to have (to God) prior to being sealed-off from Heaven at this juncture:

(Ref: Job 1:6-7)—"(6) Now there was a day when the sons of God (angels) *came to present themselves before the Lord, and Satan came also among them. (7) And the Lord said unto Satan, Where are you coming from? Then Satan answered the Lord, and said, From going to and fro in the earth, and from walking up and down in it."*

And...

(Ref: 1 Kings 22:20-22)—"(20) And the Lord said (to the angels; light and dark), *Who shall persuade Ahab, that he may go up and fall at Ramothgilead? And one said on this manner, and another said on that manner. (21) And there came forth a* (lying) *spirit, and stood before the Lord, and said, I will persuade him. (22) And the Lord said unto him, Wherewith (how)? And he said, I will go forth, and I-*(a 'dark' angel) *will be a lying spirit in the mouth of all his*

(false) *prophets. And he-(God) said, you shall persuade him, and prevail also: go forth, and do so."*

If we move across the Revelation Grid (from left to right)—(See; Fig. 3 [pg. 39]), we find that Chapter 12 revisits this Sixth Seal event; providing the more specific details of Satan's containment. **Rev 12:7-12** reads:

"(7) **And there was war in Heaven: Michael and his angels fought against the Dragon; and the Dragon fought and his angels,** *(8)* **And** (the Dragon) **prevailed not; neither was their place found any more in heaven.** *(9)* **And the great Dragon was cast out, that old Serpent, called the Devil, and Satan, which deceives the whole world: he was cast out into the earth, and his angels-**(Legion) **were cast out with him**—(See; Fig. 11 [pg. 90]). *(10)* **And I heard a loud voice saying in heaven, now is come salvation, and strength, and the kingdom of our God, and the power of his Christ—**(i.e.; 'now is come salvation' because the first of the dead/buried Saints have now been resurrected into eternal life [separated from

evil, forever], because of Jesus' victory)*: for the accuser of our brethren is cast down* (the Liar; Error)*, which accused them before our God day and night. (11) And they*-(the dead/buried Saints) *overcame him*-(Devil) *by the blood of the Lamb* (by faith in the prophecy of the Lamb, and the Lamb's subsequent victory)*, and by the word of their testimony*—(i.e.; having believed the prophecy of a Messiah [to come], and having confessed their faith [aloud] while they were alive)*; and they loved not their lives unto the death* (they did not fear [or struggle against] death, when their time came). *(12) Therefore rejoice, ye heavens, and ye that dwell in them. Woe to the inhabiters of the Earth and of the sea! for the Devil is come down unto you, having great wrath, because he knows that he hath but a short time* (to live through mankind, on Earth)— (i.e.; the Earthly realm [everything in it] is all temporary, and the Devil knows it)."

Chapter 12 goes on to describe the Devil's ever-deepening hatred for mankind (after his eviction from the Heavenlies), as well as the tools God made available to mankind (to help us endure the Devil's wrath). **Rev 12:13-17** reads:

"*(13)* ***And when the Dragon saw that he was cast unto the Earth, he persecuted the Woman-*** (prepared-mankind) ***which brought forth the man child.*** *(14)* ***And to the Woman were given two wings of a great eagle*** (the Old Testament Word and the New Testament Word), ***that she might fly into the wilderness-*** (the place of ungodliness), ***into her place, where she is nourished*** (ministered, to) ***for a time, and times, and half a time, from the face of the Serpent***—(i.e.; ministered to, until all 3 harvests are completed). *(15)* ***And the Serpent cast out of his mouth water-*** (his spirit of Evil/Error) ***as a flood after the Woman, that he might cause her to be carried away of the flood.*** *(16)* ***And the earth helped the Woman, and the earth opened her mouth, and swallowed up the flood which the Dragon cast out of his mouth***— (i.e.; the grave-[Hell] would swallow up the Whore-souls as they die, and their husband-spirits [dark angels] would once again have to return to their origin; the abyss)—(See; Fig. 11

[pg. 90]). *(17) **And the Dragon was wroth with the Woman**-*(prepared-mankind)*, **and went to make war with the Remnant of her seed** *(the faithful)*, **which keep the commandments of God** *(the Old Testament Word)*, **and have the testimony of Jesus Christ** *(the New Testament Word)."*

Roughly two thousand years have elapsed since the crucifixion and resurrection of Jesus Christ. This period has been called the 'Age-of-Grace' due to the gift of redemption Jesus bought for us (with his willing death). However, the journey has been anything but pleasant.

In summary: The first six Seals (of the Book of Seven Seals) have encapsulated the entire tumultuous history of mankind, from creation to [roughly] present-day—(i.e.; the 'things that have passed', and 'the things that are currently transpiring'). As we will see in the chapters to follow, the Seventh Seal will reveal the entire 'future' of mankind (things yet to come). The first six seals have left us running (for our lives) from a relentless and bloodthirsty adversary. At this point, you may wonder how things could possibly get any worse, for God's children —

but, as the Seventh Seal prophecy will reveal; the worst is definitely yet to come!

CHAPTER 4 — THE SEVENTH SEAL IS OPENED

The Age-of-Grace (to date) has spanned two thousand+ years. At the designated 'end' of the allotted Age-of-Grace, the Revelation tells us there will be a pause in heaven where all spiritual activity will be halted, in Heaven and on Earth — while Jesus dispatches angels to seal 144,000 (devout) souls of Israel; marking them for eventual awakening (and redemption). This preemptive census amounts to God tallying His Kingdom in preparation for immanent action. This is approximately the point at which mankind currently lives. This action will mark the beginning of the last opportunity the Lukewarm-souls will ever have, to reroute their eternal lives back toward Heaven. This is the beginning of the Sorrows-Period). **Rev 7:1-3** reads:

> "*(1) And after these things I saw four angels* (of first four trumps) *standing on the four corners of the earth, holding the four winds of the earth, that the wind should not blow on the earth, nor on the sea, nor on any tree. (2) And I saw another angel* (a 5th angel) *ascending from the east, having the seal of the living God: and he cried with a loud voice to the four angels* (with four Trumps)*, to whom it was given to hurt the earth and the sea, (3) Saying, hurt not the earth, neither the sea, nor the trees, till we have sealed the servants of our God in their foreheads.*"

This order from Heaven is the first action taken in the end-time (Seventh Seal) sequence of events. We see, in the passages above, that it is the predestined purpose of these four angels to hurt (deplete) the Earth and sea (at the onset of the Sorrows/Tribulations-Period). The passages above also reveal the presence and purpose of a fifth angel, who proceeds to find and seal 144,000 (devout) Jews, marking them (before the action starts) for redemption as the 'Last-Remnant' — just as God promised King David. Like the 'Mark of the Beast', this seal does not refer to a literal stamp on their foreheads; it will be a seal upon something in their mindset. **Rev 7:4-8** goes on, to say:

> "*(4)* **And I heard the number of them which were sealed: and there were sealed an hundred and forty and four thousand of all the tribes of the children of Israel.** *(5)* **Of the tribe of Juda were sealed twelve thousand. Of the tribe of Reuben were sealed twelve thousand. Of the tribe of Gad were sealed twelve thousand.** *(6)* **Of the tribe of Asher were sealed twelve thousand. Of the tribe of Nepthalim were sealed twelve thousand. Of the tribe of Manasses were sealed twelve thousand.** *(7)* **Of the tribe of Simeon were sealed twelve thousand. Of the tribe of Levi were sealed twelve thousand. Of the tribe of Issachar were sealed twelve thousand.** *(8)* **Of the tribe of Zabulon were sealed twelve thousand. Of the tribe of Joseph were sealed twelve thousand. Of the tribe of**

Benjamin were sealed twelve thousand." — (See;
Fig. 12 [pg. 103])

The 144,000 souls identified above (the devout of
Israel) are not being 'raptured' in this vision; they
are only being sealed by God (to be ransomed [later]
as the 'Last-Remnant'). These (devout) Jews are
obedient to the Law of God and have faith in all
prophecies of God. These 'Lost Sheep' are seen as
'blameless virgins', in God's eyes (under the Law).
The only thing they will still require (for salvation)
is the atoning blood of Jesus Christ in their hearts—
(i.e.; they're not yet convinced that Jesus was the
'Messiah' their [Old Testament] Prophecy promised
them). God will open their eyes to Jesus/Christianity
by the resurrection events of the Christian-
Witnesses/Two-Witnesses. As a result of their unbelief
at the onset of that harvest, they will miss this
particular flight out—(i.e.; the Sixth Trump harvest).
But, Jesus will come back for them (at the Seventh
Trump harvest).

Regarding the status of the Christian-
Witnesses/Two-Witnesses at this point; **Rev 7:9-10**
says:

(Fig. 12-- Witnesses Sealed)

"*(9)* **After this** (after the vision of the 144,000

being sealed [a pre-Sorrows-Period event]) **I**

beheld (another vision)**, and, lo, a great**

multitude, which no man could number (yet)*, of all nations, and kindreds, and people, and tongues, stood before the throne, and before the Lamb* (already sealed Christian-Witnesses)*, clothed with white robes* (their garment of light)*, and palms in their hands; (10) And cried with a loud voice* (ever worshipping God and Jesus)*, saying, Salvation to our God which sits upon the throne, and unto the Lamb."* — (See; Fig. 12 [pg. 103])

The above verses refer to God's 'other' flock of sheep; Christians. These verses reveal how God sees a Christianized man; wearing a white robe — perfect, through the blood of Jesus. This group cannot be numbered yet, because their final tally will not be in until the very last moment before the harvest of the Christian-Witnesses (at the Sixth Trump; end of Sorrows-Period). Consider the following verse from the book of John, which reveals a very explicit (indisputable) description of God's 'other' flock:

(Ref: John 10:16)—"And other sheep I have- (Christians)*, which are not of this fold-* (Judaism; people of the First

Covenant/amendment): *them also I must bring, and they shall hear my voice; and there shall be one fold, and one shepherd* (in eternity)."

Moving across the Revelation Grid (from left to right)—(See; Fig. 3 [pg. 39]), we find that Chapter 11 tells us God will not only inventory His people, at this time (pre-Sorrows/Tribulations-Period) — but, He will also inventory His Temple. God is measuring the players and the field, to assure that His Temple in Heaven will be filled when He is finished. **Rev 11:1-2** reads:

> "*(1) **And there was given me a reed like unto a rod: and the angel stood, saying, rise, and measure the Temple of God, and the altar** (on Earth)**, and them that worship therein** (as they stand, at this moment in time). (2) **But the court which is without the temple** (the outer courtyard) **leave out, and measure it not; for it is given unto the Gentiles** (the Non-Jewish multitudes)**: and the holy city shall they**-(the Gentiles/Non-Jewish) **tread under foot forty and two months** (3.5-years)."*

Next, God takes a moment to explain to John (a Christianized-Jew) how these non-Jewish multitudes came to be justified before His throne. He wants this confirmation on the record. **Rev 7:11-17** reads:

"*(11)* ***And all the angels stood round about the throne, and about the elders and the four Beasts, and fell before the throne on their faces, and worshipped God,*** *(12)* ***Saying, Amen: Blessing, and glory, and wisdom, and thanksgiving, and honor, and power, and might, be unto our God for ever and ever. Amen.*** *(13)* ***And one of the elders answered, saying unto me, what are these which are arrayed in white robes*** (garments of light)***?*** ***And where did they come from?*** *(14)* ***And I said unto him, Sir, you know. And he said to me, These are they which came out of great tribulation, and have washed their robes, and made them white in the blood of the Lamb***—(i.e.; Christianized souls; those willing to retain and profess the Witness of both the Law/Prophecy [Old Testament] and the Gospel of Jesus [New Testament]). *(15)* ***Therefore are they before the throne of God, and serve him day and night in his temple: and he that sits on*** *the throne shall dwell among them. (16) They shall hunger no more, neither thirst any more; neither shall the sun light on them, nor any heat. (17) For the Lamb which is in the midst of the throne shall feed them, and shall lead them unto living fountains of waters: and God shall wipe away all tears from their eyes."*

God has given mankind roughly two thousand years to master the First and Last Words (together, as a 'full' amendment) and to proclaim that full Word to all of creation. He has also 'stopped the clock' to fully assess the status of the playing field and all the players. Now, God will usher mankind into the 3.5-year Sorrows-Period (the Antichrist-uprising), which will be immediately followed by the 3.5-year Tribulations-Period (Seven Last Plagues of Wrath). At this point, the only group of mankind that has been harvested from the Earth, already, is the Early-Saints (who, have been waiting on the Sea of Glass for the past 2000+ years; waiting for the rest of God's Kingdom to join them).

During the initial 3.5-year Sorrows-Period, every Lukewarm-soul on Earth will have the opportunity to convert to Christianity (any day), and be saved. Likewise; any individual 'sheep' of Israel will have that same opportunity (any day). The Sorrows-Period will wrap up what scripture calls, the 'Summer'. The Tribulations-Period will begin the 'Winter' [Mat 24:18-21, Mar 13:14-19 & Amos 3:14-15]. **Rev 8:1-6** reads:

> "*(1)* ***And when he had opened the Seventh Seal, there was silence in Heaven about the space of half an hour.*** *(2)* ***And I saw the seven angels*** (of the Seven Churches) ***which stood before God; and to them were given seven trumpets.*** *(3)* ***And another angel*** (an 8th angel) ***came and stood at the altar, having a golden censer; and there was given unto him much incense, that he*** (the 8th angel) ***should offer it with the prayers of all saints upon the golden altar which was before the throne.*** *(4)* ***And the smoke of the incense, which came with the prayers of the saints, ascended up before God out of the angel's hand.*** *(5)* ***And the*** (8th) ***angel took the censer, and filled it with fire of the altar, and cast it into the Earth: and there were voices, and thunderings, and***

lightnings, and an earthquake. (6) And the seven angels (of the Seven Churches) *which had the seven trumpets prepared themselves to sound."*

As we will see in the verses that follow; the heavenly action described above appears to initiate a dramatic, universal 'siphoning' of anointed life-force energy/power-(3rd Part) from every corner of creation (earthly, and celestial). Here, God seems to be draining (from all pre-established reserves) the power with which He will now fill His Christian-Witnesses (empowering them for their purpose in the 3.5-year Sorrows-Period)—(See; Fig. 13 [pg. 110]). **Rev 8:7-13** goes on, to say:

"(7) The first angel sounded (First Trump of Seventh Seal)*, and there followed hail and fire mingled with blood, and they were cast upon the earth: and the third part of trees was burnt up, and all green grass was burnt up* (apparently removing anointed life-force energy/power from 3rd-Part-vegetation [as suggested by the upcoming instruction to the Fifth Angel/Trump]). *(8) And the second angel sounded* (Second Trump of Seventh Seal)*, and as it were a great mountain burning*

(Fig. 13 -- First Four Trumps)

with fire was cast into the sea: and the third
part of the sea became blood; (9) And the third
part of the creatures which were in the sea, and

had life, died (removing anointed life-force energy/power from 3rd-Part-ocean-creatures)*; and* (so) *the third part of the ships-* (vessels/'bodies') *were destroyed. (10) And the third angel sounded* (Third Trump of Seventh Seal)*, and there fell a great star from heaven, burning as it were a lamp, and it fell upon the third part of the rivers, and upon the fountains of waters; (11) And the name of the star is called Wormwood: and* (so) *the third part of the waters became Wormwood* (removing anointed life-force energy/power from 3rd-Part-rivers)*; and many men died of the waters, because they were made bitter* (men died; but no mention of river-life dying?)*. (12) And the fourth angel sounded* (Fourth Trump of Seventh Seal)*, and the third part of the sun was smitten, and the third part of the moon, and the third part of the stars; so as the third part of them was darkened, and the day shone not for a third part of it, and the night likewise* (removing anointed life-force energy/power from 3rd-Part-celestial-bodies). *(13) And I beheld, and heard an angel flying* *through the midst of heaven, saying with a loud voice, woe, woe, woe,* (three 'Woes') *to the inhabiters of the earth by reason of the other voices of the trumpets of the three angels, which are yet to sound!"* — (See; Fig. 13 [pg. 110])

CHAPTER 5 — THE SORROWS-PERIOD; ANTICHRIST UPRISING

With the angelic warnings of the Fourth Trump, Three Woes are set in place to span the seven-year Sorrows/Tribulations-Period. The Bible calls the first 3.5 years of this period the 'Beginning of Sorrows'-(aka; 'Sorrows-Period'). During the 3.5-year Sorrows-Period, the Antichrist-(Voice of Error/Evil) will steadily rise in influential power/strength—(i.e.; the First Woe), climaxing at the end of that 3.5-year-period when the fully-empowered Antichrist (Voice of Error/Evil) orchestrates the world-wide annihilation of the Christian-Witnesses/Two-Witnesses—(i.e.; the Second Woe). This movement will constitute the first Whore-Movement against the Kingdom of God (and, it will reveal the 'Man of Sin').

Throughout the Sorrows-Period, the (empowered) Christian-Witnesses will be impervious to the frenzy-tactics used by the Antichrist-(Voice of Error/Evil) to stir mankind up (like a wasp nest). **Rev 9:1-4** reads:

"(1) ***And the fifth angel sounded*** (Fifth Trump of Seventh Seal)***, and I saw a star fall from heaven unto the earth: and to him was given the key to the Bottomless Pit*** (authority)—(See; Rev 1:18). *(2)* ***And he opened the Bottomless Pit; and there arose a smoke***-(collective-Legion [of Error/Evil]; the Beast) ***out of the pit, as the smoke of a great furnace; and the sun and the air were darkened by reason of the smoke of the pit.*** *(3)* ***And there came out of the smoke locusts upon the earth: and unto them was given power, as the scorpions of the earth have power***—(i.e.; these are dark angels that will fill the Earth with poison, and devour it). *(4)* ***And it was commanded them*** (the dark Legions) ***that they should not hurt the grass of the earth, neither any green thing, neither any tree; but only those men which have not the seal of God in their foreheads***—(i.e.;

these angels are only authorized to hurt ungodly-mankind during the Sorrows-Period; not, all of creation)." — (See; Fig. 14 [pg. 116])

In the above verses, we see the action from Heaven that unleashes the Legions (of Error/Evil) that were previously imprisoned in the Pit (by the archangel, Michael). They are now given permission to roam the Earth and hurt ungodly mankind.

Moving across the Revelation Grid (from left to right)—(See; Fig. 3 [pg. 39]), we see that Chapter 11 revisits this initiation of the Sorrows-Period; detailing (this time) how God will pour into godly mankind enormous power (which He apparently siphoned from the universe, beforehand; for this purpose); making the Christian-Witnesses impervious to the chaos-tactics of the Antichrist-(Voice of Error/Evil) throughout this 3.5-year Sorrows-Period. These verses also demonstrate that the Christian-Witnesses will have both the wisdom and the authority to condemn (or, 'mark') enemies of the Kingdom of God (as; 'part of the Beast'). **Rev 11:3-5** reads:

"*(3)* ***And I will give power unto my Two Witnesses, and they shall prophesy*** (the Word of God) ***a***

(Fig. 14 -- Antichrist Uprising)

thousand two hundred and threescore days (3.5
years) **clothed in sackcloth. (4) These are the
two olive trees, and the two candlesticks** (in

right) *standing before the God of the earth*—
(i.e.; these are the faithful keepers who possess/profess 'both' lighted Words of God: the Old Testament & the New Testament). *(5)* **And if any man will hurt them**-(the Christian-Witnesses/Two-Witnesses), ***fire***-(Holy Spirit) ***proceeds out of their mouth, and devours their enemies***—(i.e.; marks & condemns them): **and if any man will hurt them** (the Christian-Witnesses), **he must in this manner be killed**—(i.e.; by Holy Spirit pouring out of Christians, in response to evil; this marks the offender and leaves all their evil on them [being unreciprocated])." —
(See; Fig. 14 [pg. 116])

Old Testament Prophecy provides a stunning portrait of the beautiful relationship between God and His two flocks (aka; the 'two candlesticks'; the 'two olive trees'-[the two Witnesses]):

(Ref: Zech 4:1-14)—"(1) And the angel that talked with me came again, and...said unto me, What do you see? And I said, I have looked, and behold a candlestick all of gold (God), *with a bowl upon the top of it* (Jesus Christ), *and his seven lamps*

thereon (the seven angels of the Seven Churches of God, on earth)*, and seven pipes to the seven lamps, which are upon the top thereof: (3) And two olive trees by it, one upon the right side of the bowl, and the other upon the left side thereof. (4) So I answered and spake to the angel that talked with me, saying....What be these two olive branches which through the two golden pipes empty the golden oil out of themselves? (13) And he answered me and said....These are the two anointed ones* (the Two Witnesses)*, that stand-*(in right standing) *by the Lord of the whole earth. "*

Moving across the Revelation Grid (from left to right)—(See; Fig. 3 [pg. 39]), we find that Chapter 13 also revisits the initiation of the Sorrows-Period; painting (instead) a picture of the Beast-(Legions of Error/Evil) rising up through Whore-souls and Lukewarm-souls to overspread the face of the earth; to blaspheme, hurt and kill. In this segment of the prophecy, this first Whore-Movement is described in terms of a powerful, destructive animal. **Rev 13:1-3** reads:

"(1) ***And I stood upon the sand of the sea, and saw a Beast*** -(collective-Legion [of Error/Evil]) ***rise up out of the sea, having seven heads*** -(seven continents) ***and ten horns, and upon his horns ten crowns*** (ten Lukewarm Kings)***, and upon his heads*** -(continents) ***the name of blasphemy.*** — (See; Fig. 14 [pg. 116]) *(2)* ***And the Beast which I saw was like unto a leopard, and his feet were as the feet of a bear, and his mouth as the mouth of a lion: and the Dragon gave him his power, and his seat, and great authority.*** *(3)* ***And I saw one of his heads*** -(continents) ***as it were wounded unto death; and his deadly wound was healed: and all the world wondered after the Beast*** -(Legions of Error/Evil)*."*

From the symbolism used above, I can easily imagine the different breeds of furious humanity that will be raging (upon the seven continents) in the end-times. I can imagine with certainty those who will be violent the way that a bear is violent (attacking in defense of themselves and their territory; feeling threatened and aggravated), as well as those who will be violent the way a lion is violent (stalking and killing to feed their bellies, and/or just to lead the pack). To my mind; the symbolism that these destroyers will only be 'members' of one single body (the solitary leopard) suggests that all destroyers of the end-time will be operating as one body and one mind (the mind of Error/Evil); in much the same way that the Body of Christ operates as one body and one mind (the mind of Truth/Goodness). As an interesting footnote; consider the following verses from the book of Psalms, which depict intriguing similarity between our seven-headed Beast, and the biblical account of God breaking up the earth into the seven continents:

> *(Ref: Psa 74:13-14)—"(13) Thou-*(God) *didst divide the sea by your strength: you broke the heads of the Dragons in the waters. (14) you broke the heads of leviathan in pieces, and gave him-*(his body and his mind) *to be meat-*(nourishment) *to the people inhabiting the wilderness* (to feed and fill the people of the Earth)."

Returning to the Revelation, **Rev 9:5-8** goes on, to say:

> *"(5)* **And to them**-(collective-Legion; the smoke from the Pit; the Beast) ***it was given that they***

should not kill them (not 'kill' the ungodly), *but that they should* (only) *be tormented five months: and their torment was as the torment of a scorpion, when he strikes a man*—(i.e.; painful and poisonous). *(6) And in those days shall men seek death, and shall not find it; and shall desire to die, and death shall flee from them. (7) And the shapes of the locusts* (devourers) *were like unto horses prepared unto battle*—(i.e.; poised for war)*; and on their heads were as it were crowns like gold* (authority)*, and their faces were as the faces of men* ('men' are what we will see when we look at this evil movement). *(8) And they had hair as the hair of women* (their minds are covered; separated, from God)*, and their teeth were as the teeth of lions."* — (See; Fig. 14 [pg. 116])

In verse 5, above, the Revelation states that this particular tormenting of the ungodly will be for a period of five months. I confess that I'm not sure what to make of that time frame. Thus far, it makes more sense to me that it may refer to the 'last' five months of the 3.5-year Sorrows-Period (where ungodly mankind finally snaps, and is driven to kill all the Christian-Witnesses on earth). It doesn't make any sense to me that they would 'begin' the period tormenting (for five months) and then stop for some reason.

Moving across the Revelation Grid (from left to right)—(See; Fig. 3 [pg. 39]); Chapter 11 revisits the power that God will have poured into the Christian-Witnesses for this 3.5-year Sorrows-Period; **Rev 11:6** reads:

> *"(6) **These** (referring to the empowered Christian-Witnesses, mentioned in Rev 11:3-5) **have power to shut heaven, that it rain not in the days of their prophecy: and have power over waters to turn them to blood, and to smite the earth with all plagues, as often as they will."** — (See; Fig. 14 [pg. 116])*

Continuing across the Revelation Grid (from left to right)—(See; Fig. 3 [pg. 39]), we see that Chapter 13 revisits the power that the Beast will have (over ungodly mankind) for this 3.5-year Sorrows-Period; **Rev 13:4-6** offers this imagery:

*"(4) **And they**-(all the world) **worshipped**-(feared and obeyed) **the Dragon**-(Father of Error/Evil) **which gave power unto the Beast: and they worshipped**-(feared and obeyed) **the Beast**-(Legions of Error/Evil), **saying, Who is like unto the Beast? who is able to make war with him?** (5) **And there was given unto him a mouth** (Whore-souls and Lukewarm-souls) **speaking great things and blasphemies; and power** (authority) **was given unto him**-(Beast/Legion of Error/Evil) **to continue forty and two months** (3.5-years). (6) **And he opened his mouth in blasphemy against God, to blaspheme his name, and his tabernacle, and them that dwell in heaven."** —* (See; Fig. 14 [pg. 116])

As suggested in verse 4, above; ungodly-(unfaithful) mankind will worship the Beast simply by virtue of fearing its growing power, and caving in to Error/Evil. This is why fear is a sin. Without Jesus (in their hearts) they are completely defenseless against the Legion (of Error/Evil); the Beast. Their fear will feed the power of the Beast, and the Beast's power will feed their fear. Therefore; as the empowered Beast rises from the Pit to flood the world,

ungodly mankind becomes engorged with Antichrist-
(Voice of Error/Evil) and that voice will ultimately
fill and overtake the world, through the Whore and the
Lukewarms. Moving down the Revelation Grid, **Rev 9:9-12**
goes on, to say:

> "*(9)* ***And they-***(Beast-driven Whore souls) ***had***
> ***breastplates*** (hearts)***, as it were breastplates of***
> ***iron; and the sound of their wings*** (their
> doctrine) ***was as the sound of chariots of many***
> ***horses running to battle*** (war). *(10)* ***And they had***
> ***tails-***(followings) ***like unto scorpions—***(i.e.;
> hurting and poisoning)***, and there were stings in***
> ***their tails: and their power was to hurt men five***
> ***months.*** *(11)* ***And they-***(Beast-driven Whore souls;
> the Whore-mindset) ***had a king over them, which is***
> ***the angel of the Bottomless Pit, whose name in***
> ***the Hebrew tongue is Abaddon, but in the Greek***
> ***tongue hath his name Apollyon.*** *(12)* ***One woe is***
> ***past—***(i.e.; the Antichrist Voice rising into
> power)***; and, behold, there come two woes more***
> ***hereafter.***" — (See; Fig. 14 [pg. 116])

According to verse 11, above; the 3.5-year
Sorrows-Period constitutes the first of Three Woes

promised to mankind. As we are about to learn; the Second Woe will be the complete annihilation of the Christian-Witnesses/Two-Witnesses (from off the face of the Earth), and the Third Woe will be the 3.5-year Tribulations-Period-(the Seven Last Plagues of Wrath). **Rev 9:13-15** reads:

> "*(13) **And the sixth angel sounded*** (Sixth Trump of Seventh Seal), ***and I heard a voice from the four horns of the golden altar which is before God, (14) Saying to the sixth angel which had the trumpet, 'loose the four angels which are bound in the great river Euphrates'. (15) And the four angels were loosed, which were prepared*** (reserved) ***for an*** (particular) ***hour, and a*** (particular) ***day, and a*** (particular) ***month, and a*** (particular) ***year, for to slay the third part of men*** (to slay the anointed Christian-Witnesses of God; the Body of Christ [the Daily Sacrifice])."
> — (See; Fig. 15 [pg. 126])

Whereas, the dark angels released from the Pit earlier (the smoke from the Pit) had been unleashed specifically upon ungodly mankind (to stir them up like a wasp nest) — note that the four angels released

(Fig. 15 -- 1st 'Whore-Movement'; Witnesses Killed)

from the Euphrates River, above, (also dark angels
from the Pit/Earth) are released specifically to
destroy the Christian-Witnesses/Two-Witnesses.

Moving across the Revelation Grid (from left to right)—(See; Fig. 3 [pg. 39]); we find that Chapter 11 defines the Two Witnesses by a testimony they have been called to proclaim to mankind. **Rev 11:7** reads:

> *"(7)* ***And when they***-(the Two Witnesses) ***shall have finished their testimony***—(i.e.; proclaiming the two lighted Words of God; First and Last Words), ***the Beast***-(Legions of Error/Evil) ***that ascends out of the Bottomless Pit*** (to indwell Whore-souls) ***shall make war against them***-(the Christian-Witnesses)*, **and shall overcome them, and kill them*** (the 2ⁿᵈ Woe)." — (See; Fig. 15 [pg. 126])

Again; it makes sense to me that this is how the Man of Sin is ultimately revealed; by causing this great falling away of the church (from off of face of the earth). Now that they have been 'revealed' (detached from the Kingdom of God) God can finally destroy them (from off the face of the Earth). Consider the overall picture painted for us by the following verses regarding this seven-year Sorrows/Tribulations-Period, in general:

(Ref: Luke 21:8-24 [& Matt 24:4-15 & Mark 13:5-20])—"(8) And he-(Jesus) said, Take heed that ye be not deceived: for many shall come in my name, saying, I am Christ; and the time draws near: go ye not therefore after them (it isn't near, yet [for the 144,000]). *(9) But when ye shall hear of wars and commotions, be not terrified: for these things must first come to pass; but the end is not by and by. (10) Then said he unto them, nation shall rise against nation, and kingdom against kingdom. (11) and great earthquakes shall be in divers places, and famines, and pestilences; and fearful sights and great signs shall there be from Heaven* (these are the beginnings of sorrows-[Mark 13:8]). *(12) But before all these* (before the end-times), *they shall lay their hands on you, and persecute you, delivering you up to the synagogues, and into prisons, being brought before kings and rulers for my name's sake. (13) And it-*(His name's sake) *shall turn to you for a testimony. (14) settle it therefore in your hearts, not to meditate before* (not to practice) *what ye shall answer. (15) For*

I will give you a mouth and wisdom, which all your adversaries shall not be able to gainsay nor resist. (16) And ye shall be betrayed both by parents, and brethren, and kinsfolks, and friends; and some of you shall they cause to be put to death. (17) And ye shall be hated of all men for my name's sake. (18) But there shall not an hair of your head perish. (19) In your patience (the Holy Spirit within) *possess ye your souls. (20) And when ye shall see Jerusalem-*(Kingdom of God) *compassed with armies* (Error/Evil standing where it ought not to be [Mark 13:14]), *then know that the desolation thereof is nigh—*(i.e.; the removal of the Kingdom of God, from earth is near). *(21) Then let them-*(of Israel) *which are in Judaea flee to the mountains; and let them which are in the midst of it-*(Judaea) *depart out; and let not them that are in the* (surrounding) *countries enter thereinto* (And let him that is on the housetop not go down into the house [to retrieve anything/anyone], *neither enter therein, to take any thing out of his house. And let him that is in the field not turn back again for to take up his garment [Mark 13:15-16]). (22) For these be the days of vengeance* (Seven Last Plagues of Wrath)*, that all things which are written may be fulfilled. (23) But woe unto them that are with child, and to them that give suck, in those days! for there shall be great distress in the land, and wrath upon this people* (And pray ye that your flight-[harvest] *be not in the winter [Mark 13:18]) (24) And they shall fall by the edge of the sword, and shall be led away captive into all nations: and Jerusalem-*(Kingdom of God) *shall be trodden down of the Gentiles, until the times of the Gentiles be fulfilled. (In those days shall be affliction, such as was not from the beginning of the creation which God created unto this time, neither shall be. And except that the Lord had shortened those days* [for the Christian-Witness harvest]*, no flesh should be saved: but for the elect's sake, whom he hath chosen, he hath shortened the days [Mark 13:19-20])."*

For centuries, pinpointing the exact timing of the 'rapture' (relative to the Tribulation period-[the

Seven Last Plagues of Wrath]) has been a source of great conjecture and debate. But, in the verse below, we find that Old Testament Prophecy painted a very clear picture of the unmistakable sequence of these end-time events; in the book of Daniel:

(Ref: Dan 9:27)—"And he shall confirm the covenant with many for one week—(i.e.; the seven year period of Sorrows & Tribulations)*: and in the midst of the week* (at the 3.5-year mark) *he shall cause the* (daily) *sacrifice and the oblation to cease*—(i.e.; cause the Christian-Witnesses/*servants* on Earth to be killed, after 3.5 years)*, and for the overspreading of abominations he shall make it desolate* (void of Kingdom-Seed, for 3 whole days)*, even until the consummation* (when the Kingdom-Seed is rained back down, to feed the 144,000 [during the resurrection of the Christian-Witnesses])*, and that determined shall be poured upon the desolate* (poured upon the godless Earth)*."*

And...

(Ref: Dan 11:31-36)—"(31) And arms (authoritative armies) *shall stand on his part, and they shall*

pollute the sanctuary of strength (the physical bodies-[temples] of God)*, and shall take away the daily sacrifice* (by killing the servants of the Kingdom of God; the Christian-Witnesses)*, and they shall place the abomination that maketh desolate* (the armies [of Error] surrounding Jerusalem-[the Kingdom of God])*. (32) And such as do wickedly against the covenant* (willing sinners) *shall he corrupt by flatteries: but the people that do know their God* (the Kingdom of God) *shall be strong, and do exploits. (33) And they that understand* (Christian teachers) *among the people shall instruct many: yet they shall fall by the sword, and by flame, by captivity, and by spoil, many days. (34) Now when they shall fall, they shall be helped with a little help: but many shall cleave to them with flatteries* (trying to corrupt them)*. (35) And some of them of understanding shall fall, to try them, and to purge, and to make them white* (being completed in their last moments of life)*, even to the time of the end: because it is yet for a time appointed. (36) And the king-*(Error in charge; Antichrist spirit) *shall do according to his will; and he shall exalt himself, and magnify himself above every god, and shall speak marvelous things against the God of gods, and shall prosper till the indignation be accomplished: for that that is determined shall be done* (it is preordained to be)."

In the above verses, we are told that there will be a seven-year period in which God will work to confirm salvation with many souls. Also; that in the middle of that seven-year period, the Two Witnesses-(Body of Christ; Daily Sacrifice) will be removed, leaving the Earth desolate of Kingdom-Seed for three whole days (until God rains back down a 'consummation' of Kingdom-Seed to feed the 144,000/Remnant; to open their eyes, to Jesus). The 144,000 will be harvested 3.5 years later (at the end of the seven-year Sorrows/Tribulations-Period).

Continuing across the Revelation Grid (from left to right)—(See; Fig. 3 [pg. 39]), we see that Chapter 13 also revisits the destruction of the Christian-Witnesses/Two-Witnesses; shining a spotlight on the power and influence of the Beast during this first Whore-Movement. **Rev 13:7-10** reads:

"*(7) And it was given unto him*-(Beast; Legions of Error/Evil) *to make war with the saints, and to overcome them: and power was given him over all kindreds, and tongues, and nations. (8) And all* (ungodly) *that dwell upon the earth shall worship*-(fear and obey) *him, whose names are not written in the book of life of the Lamb slain from the foundation of the world. (9) If any man have an ear, let him hear. (10) He that leads into captivity shall go into captivity: he that kills with the sword must be killed with the sword. Here is the patience and the faith of the saints.*" — (See; Fig. 15 [pg. 126])

Moving down and across the Revelation Grid (from left to right)-(See; Fig. 3 [pg. 39]); Chapter 9 continues its description of the army that overtakes the Christian-Witnesses.

(**Rev 9:16-17** goes on, to say):

"*(16) And the number of the army of the horsemen were two hundred thousand thousand: and I heard the number of them. (17) And thus I saw the horses* (power) *in the vision, and them* (the Whore souls) *that sat on them, having breastplates* (hearts) *of fire, and of jacinth, and brimstone* (hatred)*: and the heads* (minds) *of the horses were as the heads* (minds) *of lions; and out of their mouths* (the horse's mouths) *issued fire and smoke and brimstone."* — (See; Fig. 15 [pg. 126])

It is during this first Whore-Movement (at the end of the 3.5-year Sorrows-Period) that we see our first glimpse of the 'Authoritative' Antichrist-(Voice of Error/Evil); when that voice (through the Beast and through the Whore) overcomes and kills the Christian-Witnesses-(the Body of Christ). Moving across the Revelation Grid (from left to right)—(See; Fig. 3 [pg. 39]), we see that Chapter 13 goes on to offer a detailed description of the Authoritative Antichrist. **Rev 13:11-12** reads:

"(11) And I beheld another (stronger) *Beast coming up out of the earth* (having the 'Authoritative' Voice of Error; the fully-empowered Antichrist)*; and he had two horns like a lamb* (gained his power in the name of peace)*, and he spake as a Dragon* (in Error)*. (12) And he*

exercises all the power of (gained by) *the first Beast before him, and causes* (forces) *the earth and them which dwell therein to worship*-(fear and obey) *the first Beast*-(who laid the groundwork of Error/Evil)*, whose deadly wound was healed*—(i.e.; Authoritative Antichrist Voice causes them to worship the original groundwork of Error [which, is apparently subdued at some point, but comes back in full-force])*."* — (See; Fig. 15 [pg. 126]) Chapter 13 goes on, to say, in **Rev 13:13-18**:

"(13) **And he**-('Authoritative' Voice of Error; the fully-empowered Antichrist [2nd Beast]) *doeth great wonders, so that he maketh fire come down from heaven on the earth in the sight of men,*

(14) **And deceives them that dwell on the earth by the means of those miracles which he had power to do in the sight of the Beast; saying to them that dwell on the earth** (the Lukewarms, and the 144,000) *that they should make an image to the Beast* (become like him)*, which had the wound by a sword, and did live*—(i.e.; forcing them to become like the Beast [become Whores of Error/Evil] if they want to survive)*. (15)* **And he**-

('Authoritative' Voice of Error; the fully-empowered Antichrist [2nd Beast]) *had power to give life unto the image of the Beast* (had power to make new Whores), *that the image of the Beast* (the Whore souls) *should both speak, and cause that as many as would not worship*-(fear and obey) *the image of the Beast, should be killed*—(i.e.; that everyone who refused to become a 'Whore' would be killed by the Whores). *(16)* *And he*-(Authoritative Voice of Error; the fully-empowered Antichrist [2nd Beast]) *caused all, both small and great, rich and poor, free and bond, to receive a mark in their right hand, or in their foreheads*—(i.e.; the Voice of Error/Evil [Antichrist] forces mankind to think corruptly [with their head] and act corruptly [by work of their hands] against the people of God, just to survive — which marks them as 'part of the Beast']). *(17)* *And that no man might buy or sell, save he that had the mark, or the name of the Beast, or the number of his name*—(i.e.; that a man could no longer survive, outside of corruption). *(18)* *Here is wisdom. Let him that hath understanding count the number of the Beast* (number of Legion)*: for it is the number of* (Legion, within) *a man; and his number is Six hundred threescore and six."* — (See; Fig. 15 [pg. 126])

It is extremely important, in this instance, that we be willing to consider other biblical uses of the word 'mark' (aside from thinking of it as a literal 'stamp' on something); Consider the following passage:

(Ref: Rom 16:16-17)—"(16) Salute one another with an holy kiss. The churches of Christ salute you. (17) Now I beseech you, brethren, mark them which cause divisions and offences contrary to the doctrine which ye have learned; and avoid them— (i.e.; separate yourselves from people 'marked by' offending and/or dividing the people of God; honoring false doctrine-[Error])*."*

The above verse suggests that when a man receives the mark of ungodliness (the Mark of the Beast), it is a mark 'assessed' to him (by the judgement of Godly mankind; having observed his mindset and the activities of his hands). This 'marking' is not as though the soul stands in line to be literally stamped on his forehead, or, holds out his hand to receive a mark (as at a nightclub, etc...). I believe God's last (strenuous) warning for us to avoid the mark of the Beast can be translated more simply; "Do not cave into the voice of Error, resorting to evil tactics to survive or thrive during these difficult days (in particular; do not cause harm to the Kingdom of God) because it will mark you as part of the Beast."

Indeed, not only the Whore will be marked [by her willing marriage to the Beast], but also the weak soul who simply fears and obeys (worships) the Whore, will be marked. Consider the following additional verses that seem to support the presupposition that it is our 'mindset' and/or the 'activities of our hands' (rather than a stamp on our forehead or hands) that will mark a man as part of the Beast:

(Ref: Rev 14:9)—"And the third angel followed them, saying with a loud voice, If any man worship-(fear and obey) *the Beast-*(Legions of Error/Evil) *and his image-*(his Whore-bride)*, and receive his mark in his forehead, or in his hand* (being assessed as an offense against the Word of God or His people, by their mindset or by the

activity of their hands]), *The same shall drink of the wine of the wrath of God..."*

And...

(Ref: Rev 14:11)—"And the smoke of their torment ascends up for ever and ever: and they have no rest day nor night, who worship-(fear and obey) *the Beast-*(Legions of Error/Evil) *and his image-*(his Whore-bride), *and whosoever receives the mark of his name* (being assessed as an offense against the Word of God or His people, by their mindset or by their behavior])."

And...

(Ref: Rev 15:2)—"And I saw as it were a Sea of Glass mingled with fire: and them that had gotten the victory over the Beast, and over his image, and over his mark, and over the number of his name—(i.e.; he saw them that were not assessed as an offense against the Word of God or His people [by their mindset or behavior], nor feared and obeyed the Whore), *stand on the Sea of Glass, having the harps of God."*

And...

(Ref: Rev 16:2)—*"And the first* (angel) *went, and poured out his vial upon the earth; and there fell a noisome and grievous sore upon the men which had the mark of the Beast-*(Error/Evil)*, and upon them which worshipped-*(feared and obeyed) *his image-*(his Whore-bride)*—*(i.e.; there fell a sore upon the Whore [men who have been assessed as an offense against the Word of God or His people, by their mindset or behavior] and upon those who fear and obey them)*."*

And...

(Ref: Rev 19:20)—*"And the Beast-*(Legions of Error/Evil) *was taken, and with him the false prophet* (the Antichrist-[Voice of Error/Evil]) *that wrought miracles before him, with which he deceived them that had received the mark of the Beast—*(i.e.; them that had been assessed as an offense against the Word of God or His people [by their mindset or behavior])*, and them that worshipped-*(feared and obeyed) *his image-*(his Whore-bride)*. These both* (Beast-[Legions of Error/Evil] and Antichrist-[Voice of Error/Evil])

were cast alive into a lake of fire burning with brimstone."

And...

(Ref: Rev 20:4)—"And I saw thrones, and they sat upon them, and judgment was given unto them: and I saw the souls of them that were beheaded for the Witness of Jesus, and for the Word of God, and which had not worshipped-(feared and obeyed) *the Beast-*(Legions of Error/Evil)*, neither his image-*(his Whore-bride)*, neither had received his mark upon their foreheads, or in their hands* (hadn't been assessed as an offense against the Word of God or His people [by their mindset or behavior])*..."*

Returning to the Revelation; Chapter 9 describes the hatred that will be at the core of killing the Witnesses; **Rev 9:18-19** reads:

"(18) **By these three** (fire, smoke & brimstone) **was the third part of men** (the Christian-Witnesses) **killed, by the fire, and by the smoke, and by the brimstone** (the heart power; hatred), **which issued out of their mouths.** *(19)* **For their power is in their mouth-**(words)**, and in their**

tails-(their following)—(i.e.; their power is in their seducing words and in the sheer numbers of their mob-following)*: for their Tails*-(following) *were like unto Serpents*-(Error/Evil)*, and had heads*-(accommodating minds/wills)*, and with them they do hurt."* — (See; Fig. 15 [pg. 126])

Moving across the Revelation Grid (from left to right)—(See; Fig. 3 [pg. 39]), we find that Chapter 11 also revisits the slaughter of the Christian-Witnesses; focusing on what becomes of their dead bodies after they are killed. **Rev 11:8-10** adds:

"(8) And their dead bodies (the Christian-Witnesses) *shall lie in the street of the great city*-(the Evil World; Babylon [See Rev 16:19-21])*, which spiritually is called Sodom and Egypt, where also our Lord was crucified. (9) And they of the people and kindreds and tongues and nations* (the Whore and the Lukewarms) *shall see their dead bodies three days and a half* (lying in the streets for 3.5 days)*, and shall not suffer their dead bodies to be put in graves. (10) And they that dwell upon the earth* (Whore and Lukewarm) *shall rejoice over them* (dead

Christian-Witnesses), *and make merry, and shall send gifts one to another; because these two prophets* (keepers of the First and Last Words) *tormented them*-(the ungodly) *that dwelt on the earth.*" — (See; Fig. 15 [pg. 126])

And so; at the end of the 3.5-year Sorrows-Period, the stirred-up Whore-(collective-soul of mankind that blasphemes Truth/Good; preferring the convenience of Error/Evil) will lash out at the Christian-Witnesses and kill them. As yet, the Lukewarms have neither blasphemed the Holy Spirit of Truth, nor, partnered with the Whore to destroy the Kingdom of God. They have, therefore, not yet been assessed as 'part of the Beast'. Albeit: the Whore and the Lukewarms will celebrate the absence of the Christian-Witnesses vigorously (because they are all convinced that the stifling demands of Christian principals are responsible for much world conflict). Consider the following verses, which add further insight to this end-time scenario:

(Ref: Jer 25:32-37)—"(32) Thus says the Lord of hosts, Behold, Evil shall go forth from nation to nation, and a great whirlwind shall be raised up

from the coasts of the earth. (33) And the slain of the Lord (the Christian-Witnesses) *shall be at that day from one end of the earth even unto the other end of the earth: they shall not be lamented, neither gathered, nor buried; they shall be dung upon the ground. (34) Howl, ye shepherds-*(Christians)*, and cry; and wallow yourselves in the ashes, ye principal of the flock-*(the 144,000)*: for the days of your slaughter and of your dispersions-*(the rain of Kingdom-Seed; to feed the 144,000) *are accomplished; and ye shall fall like a pleasant vessel* (not fighting back)*. (35) And the shepherds-*(Christian-Witnesses) *shall have no way to flee, nor the principal of the flock-*(the 144,000)*: to escape. (36) A voice of the cry of the shepherds, and an howling of the principal of the flock, shall be heard: for the Lord hath spoiled their pasture. (37) And the peaceable habitations are cut down because of the fierce anger of the Lord."*

CHAPTER 6 — THE HARVEST OF THE TWO WITNESSES

Chapter 11 goes on to tell us that after lying dead in the streets for three days, the Christian-Witnesses will finally be harvested to the Sea of Glass, where they will immediately begin to minister to the (newly awakened) 144,000/Remnant (who will remain on earth, throughout the Tribulations-Period [on Mt. Zion])—(See; Fig. 10[b] [pg. 148]). These Chapter 11 verses tell us that an overflow of Kingdom-Seed will be recouped through the Christian-Witnesses' harvest event — and, that God will immediately rain that recouped Seed back down to Earth (into the 144,000/Remnant; to open their eyes to Jesus); **Rev 11:11-13** reads:

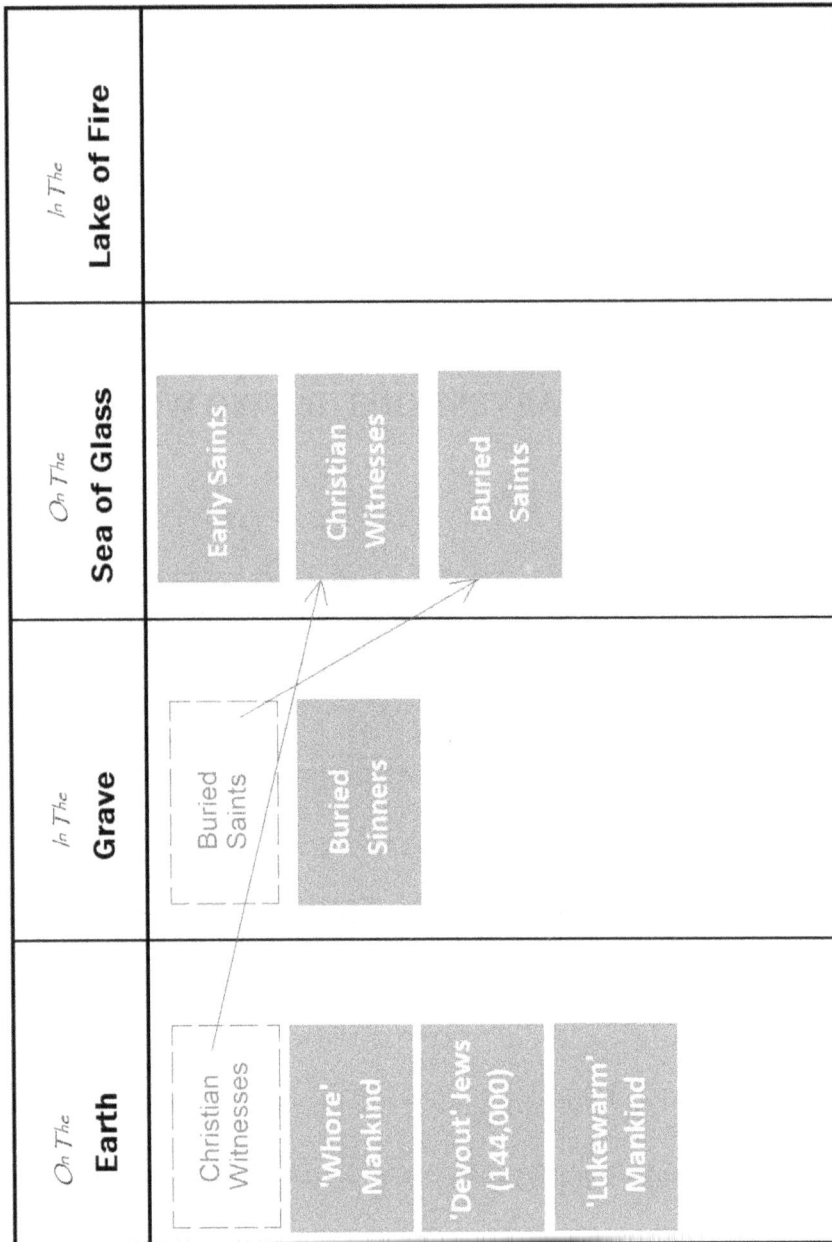

(Fig. 10b -- Christian Witnesses [and Buried Saints] Harvested to Sea of Glass)

"(11) **And after three days and a half**-(3.5 days)

the Spirit of life (life-force energy/power) **from**

God entered into them (into the dead bodies of

the Christian-Witnesses), **and they** (the enlivened

bodies/souls) *stood upon their feet; and great fear fell upon them which saw them. (12) And they heard a great voice from heaven saying unto them, Come up hither. And they-*(the enlivened bodies/souls of the Christian-Witnesses) *ascended up to Heaven in a cloud; and their enemies beheld them. (13) And the same hour was there a great earthquake, and the tenth part of the city*-(i.e.; the overflow of harvested Kingdom-Seed) *fell* (rained back down onto earth, to feed/awaken the 144,000/Remnant)*, and in the earthquake were slain of men seven thousand: and the Remnant-* (144,000 devout Jews) *were affrighted, and gave glory to the God of heaven*-(i.e.; the 144,000 were awakened, and finally acknowledged/accepted Jesus as God's son; the 'Messiah')." — (See; Fig. 16 [pg. 150])

The verses above do not mention that 'all' of the dead/buried saints are also going to be raised from their graves at this time (during the death/resurrection of the Christian-Witnesses), but they are going to be; the earthquake breaks open their graves, and they rise, too. Consider the following

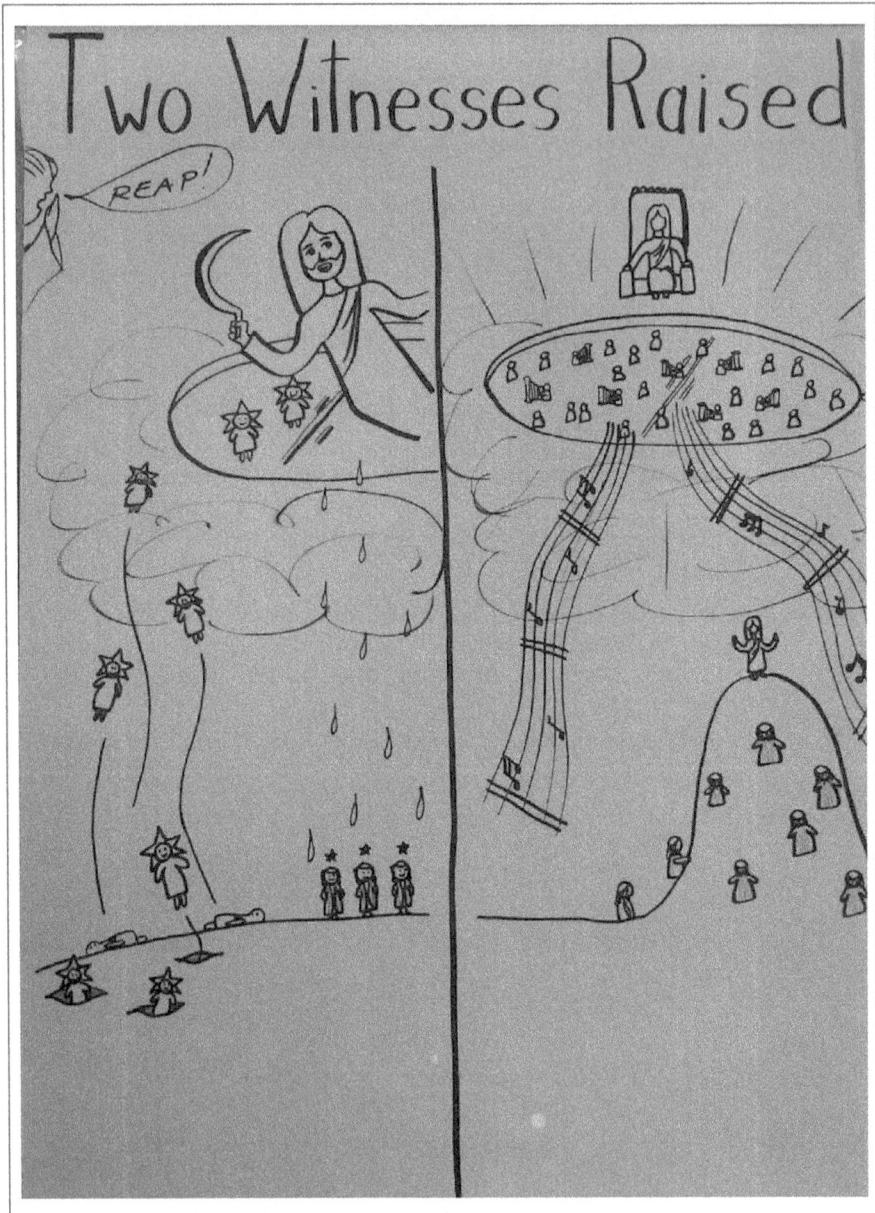

(Fig. 16 -- Witnesses Harvested)

verses which detail the order in which the dead will be raised in the end-time harvests:

(Ref: 1 Thes 4:13-17)—"(13) But I would not have you to be ignorant, brethren, concerning them which are asleep-(dead/lifeless)*...(15) For this we-*(the Christianized-Jew Apostles) *say unto you by the word of the Lord, that we which are alive and remain unto the* (second) *coming of the Lord—*(i.e.; the 'end-time' 144,000/Remnant of Israel) *shall not prevent them which are asleep* (those who are dead and/or buried) (from rising).*(16) For the Lord himself shall descend* (hover) *from heaven with a shout, with the voice of the archangel* (Michael), *and with the* (6th) *trump of God: and the dead in Christ* (the Christian-Witnesses & all dead/buried Saints/Christians) *shall rise first* (at the Sixth Trump harvest): *(17) Then we* (of Israel) *which are alive and remain* (the 144,000/Remnant) *shall be caught up* (in the 'twinkling of an eye') *together with them in the clouds* (at the Seventh Trump harvest), *to meet the Lord in the air: and so shall we ever be with the Lord."*

Interestingly; in Rev. 11:13 (above), we also saw vague mention of seven thousand (additional) souls who are killed during the resurrection of the Christian-Witnesses (for reasons left undisclosed). Might these seven thousand souls relate (in some way) to the seven thousand souls God said He 'reserved for Himself' when He ordered Israel's destruction in the desert (*1 King 19:14-18*)? Does this have something to do with how God gets the extra Kingdom-Seed in the end-time? Consider the end of this Old Testament passage:

(Ref: 1 King 19:14-18)—" (14) And he said, I-(the prophet, Elijah) *have been very jealous for the Lord God of hosts: because the children of Israel have forsaken thy covenant, thrown down thine altars, and slain thy prophets with the sword; and I, even I only, am left; and they seek my life, to take it away* (this, under the rule of Ahab and Jezebel). *(15) And the Lord said unto him, Go, return on thy way to the wilderness of Damascus: and when you come, anoint Hazael to be king over Syria: (16) And Jehu the son of Nimshi shalt thou anoint to be king over Israel: and Elisha the son of Shaphat of Abelmeholah shalt thou anoint to be prophet in thy room. (17) And it shall come to pass, that him-*(of Israel) *that*

escapes the sword of Hazael-(King of Syria) *shall* (King) *Jehu slay: and him that escapes from the sword of* (King) *Jehu shall Elisha-*(Elijah's apprentice-prophet) *slay. (18) Yet I have left me seven thousand in Israel, all the knee which have not bowed unto Baal, and every mouth which hath not kissed him."*

Moving across the Revelation Grid (from left to right)—(See; Fig. 3 [pg. 39]), we see that Chapter 14 revisits the harvest of the Christian-Witnesses; offering a more detailed image of Jesus summoning the resurrected Christian-Witnesses (and the buried dead) up into Heaven; **Rev 14:14-16** reads:

"(14) **And I looked, and behold a white cloud, and upon the cloud one sat like unto the Son of Man, having on his head a golden crown** (the risen Jesus)**, and in his hand a sharp sickle.** *(15)* **and another angel came out of the temple, crying with a loud voice to him that sat on the cloud, thrust in your sickle, and reap: for the time is come for you to reap; for the harvest of the earth is ripe.** *(16)* **And he that sat on the cloud** (the risen Jesus) **thrust in his sickle on the earth;**

and the Earth was reaped (the dead Christian-Witnesses and Saints were raised into heaven)." — (See; Fig. 16 [pg. 150])

Consider these Old Testament prophecies regarding the harvest of the Christian-Witnesses:

(Ref: Isa 6:11-13)—"*(11) Then said I, Lord, how long? And he answered, Until the cities*-(the Kingdom of God) *be wasted without inhabitant, and the houses*-(fleshen bodies) *without man*-(without Seed of God)*, and the land be utterly desolate* (of God's people)*, (12) And the Lord have removed men far away* (removed the children of God to the Sea of Glass)*, and there be a great forsaking* (of the people of God) *in the midst of the land. (13) But yet in it* (in the 'great forsaking'; in the harvest) *shall be a tenth* (part)*, and it shall return* (the rain of Kingdom-Seed)*, and shall be eaten* (by the 144,000)*: as a teil tree, and as an oak, whose substance*-(likeness) *is in them, when they cast their leaves: so the Holy Seed shall be the substance thereof*—(i.e.; the Holy Seed shall become the 'substance' of the 144,000/Remnant)." And...

(Ref: Isa 10:22-23)—"(22) For though your people Israel be as the sand of the sea, yet a Remnant of them shall return: the consumption (the feeding of Kingdom-Seed) *decreed shall overflow with righteousness—*(i.e.; have extra). *(23) For the Lord God of hosts shall make a consumption* (a feeding)*, even determined, in the midst of all the land."*

And...

(Ref: Isa 27:5-6)—"(5) Or let him-(the Gentile/ungodly) *take hold of my strength* (Jesus)*, that he may make peace with me; and he shall make peace with me. (6) He-*(the Christianized gentile) *shall cause-*(facilitate) *them that come of Jacob* (the 144,000) *to take root* (in the end-time)*: Israel shall blossom and bud, and fill the face of the world with fruit—* (i.e.; they shall become productive servants of God, again)."

And...

Ref: (Isa 30:19-23)—"(19) For the people- (144,000/Remnant of Israel) *shall dwell in Zion at Jerusalem: you shall weep no more: he-*(Lord)

will be very gracious unto you at the voice of
your cry; when he shall hear it, he will answer
you. *(20) And though the Lord give you the bread
of adversity, and the water of affliction* (the
Tribulations-Period), *yet shall not your teachers
be removed into a corner any more, but thine eyes
shall see your teachers* (the immortalized
Christian-Witnesses)*: (21) And thine ears shall
hear a Word behind you, saying, this is the way,
walk ye in it, when ye turn to the right hand,
and when ye turn to the left. (22) Ye shall
defile also the covering of your graven images of
silver* (discarding them)*, and the ornament of
your molten images of gold: you shall cast them
away as a menstruous cloth; you shall say unto
it, Get you hence. (23) then shall he give the
rain of your Seed, that you shall sow the ground
withal; and bread of the increase of the earth,
and it shall be fat and plenteous: in that day
shall your cattle feed in large pastures."*
And...

*(Ref: Dan 9:27)—"And he shall confirm the
covenant with many for one week—*(i.e.; the seven-

year period of Sorrows/Tribulations): *and in the midst of the week* (at the 3.5-year mark) *he shall cause the* (daily) *sacrifice and the oblation to cease* (the Christian-Witnesses/servants will be killed)*, and for the overspreading of abominations he shall make it desolate*—(i.e.; completely void of God's Seed, for 3 whole days)*, even until the consummation*-(when the Kingdom-Seed is rained back down, to feed/awaken the 144,000)*, and that determined shall be poured upon the desolate* (on ungodly earth)."

Moving down and across the Revelation Grid, Chapter 14 goes on to describe how the raised Christian-Witnesses (now in Heaven, on the Sea of Glass) will immediately begin ministering (singing and playing harps) to the 144,000 still 'mortal' Remnant on Mt. Zion. In the verses below, this time of ministering is described from an earthly point of view; **Rev 14:1-2** reads:

"(1) ***And I looked, and, lo, a Lamb***-(Jesus) ***stood on the mount Sion***-(Mt. Zion)*,* ***and with him an hundred forty and four thousand***-(144,000 still mortal Jews)*,* ***having his father's name***-('Savior')

written in their foreheads—(i.e.; the 144,000 who's mindset now embraces Jesus as 'Messiah').

(2) ***And I heard a voice from heaven, as the voice of many waters, and as the voice of a great thunder: and I heard the voice of harpers harping with their harps*** (heard the immortalized Christians and Early-Saints [on Sea of Glass] ministering to the 144,000/Remnant [on Earth], to strengthen them)*:"* — (See; Fig. 16 [pg. 150])

Continuing across the Revelation Grid (from left to right)—(See; Fig. 3 [pg. 39]), we see that Chapter 15 revisits the scenario of the raised Witnesses ministering to the 144,000 on Earth; but this time, from the perspective of Heaven. **Rev 15:2-4** reads:

"(2) ***And I saw as it were a Sea of Glass mingled with fire: and them that had gotten the victory over the Beast*** (Error/Evil)***, and over his image, and over his mark, and over the number of his name*** (the raised Witnesses and Saints)***, stand on the Sea of Glass, having the harps of God.*** *(3)* ***And they sing the Song of Moses the servant of God*** (the First Word; Old Testament)***, and*** (they sing) ***the Song of the Lamb*** (the Last Word; New

Testament), *saying, Great and marvelous are your works, Lord God Almighty; just and true are your ways, you King of saints. (4) Who shall not fear you, O Lord, and glorify your name? for you only are holy: for all nations shall come and worship before you; for your judgments are made manifest.*" — (See; Fig. 16 [pg. 150])

Rev 14:3-5 goes on, to say:

"*(3) And they*-(the resurrected Christians and Early-Saints) *sung as it were a new song* (teaching the [still mortal] 144,000/Remnant the ways of Jesus) *before the throne, and before the four Beasts, and the elders* (singing, from the Sea of Glass)*: and no man* (on Earth) *could learn that song but*-(except) *the hundred and forty and four thousand* (the Remnant)*, which were redeemed from the earth* ('saved')*. (4) These are they which were not defiled with women; for they are virgins* (according to the Law of God)*. These are they which follow the Lamb*-(Jesus) *whithersoever he goes* (having been awakened during the Christian harvest events)*. These were redeemed from among men, being the firstfruits unto God*

(per Law) **and to the Lamb** (per Grace). (These are
the first souls to be considered fruit to God
'and' to Jesus [rather than, to one or the
other]; they are fruits to God under the Law
[because they broke no law of God, in His eyes],
and they are fruits to Jesus under Grace [because
Jesus now lives inside their hearts]. As such;
these 144,000 are the first to be fruits to
'both' God and Jesus.) *(5)* **And in their mouth was
found no guile: for they** (the 144,000) **are
without fault before the throne of God."** — (See;
Fig. 16 [pg. 150])

In verse 3, above, the Revelation says that
immediately after the Christian-Witnesses are
harvested (and begin ministering [singing the songs of
Moses and Jesus] to the 144,000), the Whore and the
Lukewarm will not be able (or, willing) to learn the
song of Jesus; only the 144,000/Remnant can learn that
song, from this point forward. In other words; no
other souls will ever come to Jesus, from this point
forward (after the Christian-Witnesses are
resurrected; end of Sorrows-Period). For the next 3.5
years (throughout the subsequent Tribulations-Period-

[Seven Last Plagues of Wrath]), the immortalized Christian-Witnesses and Saints will minister to the still mortal 144,000/Remnant; strengthening their new-found Christianity. Consider the following verses, which give additional insight to the longsuffering love of God toward the 144,000 He redeems from Israel (based on something special that was present in their mindset at the moment He sent His angels to seal them):

> *(Ref: Jer 23:3-8)—"(3) And I will gather the Remnant of my flock* (the 144,000) *out of all countries whither I have driven them, and will bring them again to their folds; and they shall be fruitful and increase* (producing fruit of the spirit on Mt. Zion during Tribulations-Period). *(4) And I will set up shepherds over them which shall feed them—*(i.e.; the immortalized Christian-Witnesses, ministering to the 144,000/Remnant): *and they shall fear no more, nor be dismayed, neither shall they be lacking, says the Lord...the days come, says the Lord, that they shall no more say, The Lord lives, which brought up the children of Israel out of*

the land of Egypt; (8) But, The Lord lives, which brought up and which led the Seed of the house of Israel (the anointed 144,000) *out of the north country, and from all countries whither I had driven them; and they shall dwell in their own land."*

And...

(Ref: Jer 3:14-15)—"(14) Turn, O backsliding children, says the Lord; for I am married unto you: and I will take you one of a city, and two of a family (only the devout), *and I will bring you to Zion: (15) And I will give you pastors-* (immortalized Christian teachers) *according to mine heart* (providing the heart-amendment), *which shall feed you with knowledge and understanding."*

And...

(Ref: Isa 29:24)—"They also that erred in spirit (the 144,000) *shall come to understanding, and they that murmured shall learn doctrine* (the 144,000 will study and learn the Gospel/doctrine of Jesus)."

And...

(Ref: Isa 30:29)—"Ye-(the 144,000) shall have a song, as in the night when a holy solemnity is kept; and gladness of heart, as when one goes with a pipe to come into the mountain of the Lord, to the mighty One of Israel."

And...

(Ref: Ezek 34:12-16)—"(12) As a shepherd seeks out his flock in the day that he is among his sheep that are scattered; so will I seek out my (peaceful) *sheep, and will deliver them out of all places where they have been scattered in the cloudy and dark day. (13) And I will bring them out from the people, and gather them from the countries, and will bring them to their own land, and feed them upon the mountains of Israel by the rivers, and in all the inhabited places of the country. (14) I will feed them in a good pasture, and upon the high mountains of Israel shall their fold be: there shall they lie in a good fold, and in a fat pasture shall they feed upon the mountains of Israel. (15) I will feed my flock, and I will cause them to lie down, says the Lord God. (16) I will seek that which was lost, and*

bring again that which was driven away, and will bind up that which was broken, and will strengthen that which was sick: but I will destroy the fat and the strong; I will feed them with judgment."

And...

(Ref: Jer 33:6-11)—"(6) Behold, I will bring it- (the Remnant) *health and cure, and I will cure them* (complete them)*, and will reveal unto them the abundance of Peace and Truth* (New Testament Gospel)*. (7) And I will cause the captivity of Judah and the captivity of Israel to return, and will build them, as at the first. (8) And I will cleanse them from all their iniquity, whereby they have sinned against me; and I will pardon all their iniquities, whereby they have sinned, and whereby they have transgressed against me. (9) And it shall be to me a name of joy, a praise and an honor before all the nations of the earth, which shall hear all the good that I do unto them: and they shall fear and tremble for all the Goodness and for all the prosperity that I procure unto it. (10) Thus says the Lord; Again*

there shall be heard in this place, which ye say shall be desolate without man and without Beast, even in the cities of Judah, and in the streets of Jerusalem, that are desolate, without man, and without inhabitant, and without Beast, (11) The voice of joy, and the voice of gladness, the voice of the Bridegroom-(Jesus)*, and the voice of the Bride-*(collective-soul of Godly mankind)*, the voice of them that shall say, Praise the Lord of hosts: for the Lord is good; for his mercy endures for ever: and of them that shall bring the sacrifice of praise into the house of the Lord. For I will cause to return the captivity of the land, as at the first, says the Lord."*

In review: The Early-Saints had been harvested from the Earth (to the Sea of Glass) on the same day that Jesus ascended into Heaven (two thousand+ years ago). And now, a second part of the Body of Christ has also been harvested from the Earth to the Sea of Glass (the slain Christian-Witnesses [along with all previously-buried Christians and Saints]). This leaves (alive on Earth) only the 144,000/Remnant, the Whore-(Gog), and the Lukewarms-(Magog), and the earthly

grave-(Hell) now holds only the dead/buried damned. —
(See; Fig. 10[b] [pg. 148]).

The verses below go on to tell us there won't be
one more soul who will ever repent, from this point
forward—(i.e.; from the point where the Witnesses are
harvested and the 144,000 come to Jesus). The Whore-
mindset has already made its eternal decision to
partner with Error/Evil, and those of the Lukewarm-
mindset will eventually also 'marry' themselves to
Error/Evil (at the end of the 1,000-Year-Reign).

Returning to the Revelation (picking up just
after the Christian-Witnesses are harvested); **Rev
9:20-21** reads:

> "*(20)* ***And the rest of the men which were not
> killed by these plagues*** (the violent and chaotic
> events of the Sorrows-Period) ***yet repented not of
> the works*** (activities) ***of their hands, that they
> should not worship*** (fear and obey) ***Devils, and
> idols of gold, and silver, and brass, and stone,
> and of wood: which neither can see, nor hear, nor
> walk: (21) neither repented they of their
> murders, nor of their sorceries, nor of their
> fornication, nor of their thefts***—(i.e.; the

ungodly men still would not repent of their evil mindset)."

As the immortalized Christian-Witnesses and Early-Saints (on the Sea of Glass) begin ministering to the 144,000/Remnant (on Mt. Zion), God also sends several ministering angels to issue warnings to them. **Rev 10:1-3** reads:

> "*(1) **And I saw another mighty angel come down from heaven, clothed with a cloud: and a rainbow was upon his head, and his face was as it were the sun, and his feet as pillars of fire.** (2) **And He had in his hand a little book open: and he set his right foot upon the sea, and his left foot on the earth,** (3) **And cried with a loud voice, as when a lion roars: and when he had cried, seven thunders uttered their voices.**" — (See; Fig. 17 [pg. 168])

Earlier, we saw that the 'rising' of the Antichrist-(Voice of Error/Evil) was referred to as the 'First Woe'-(i.e.; the Sorrows-Period). Moving across the Revelation Grid (from left to right)—(See; Fig. 3 [pg. 39]), we see in Chapter 11 that the killing of the Christian-Witnesses (by the

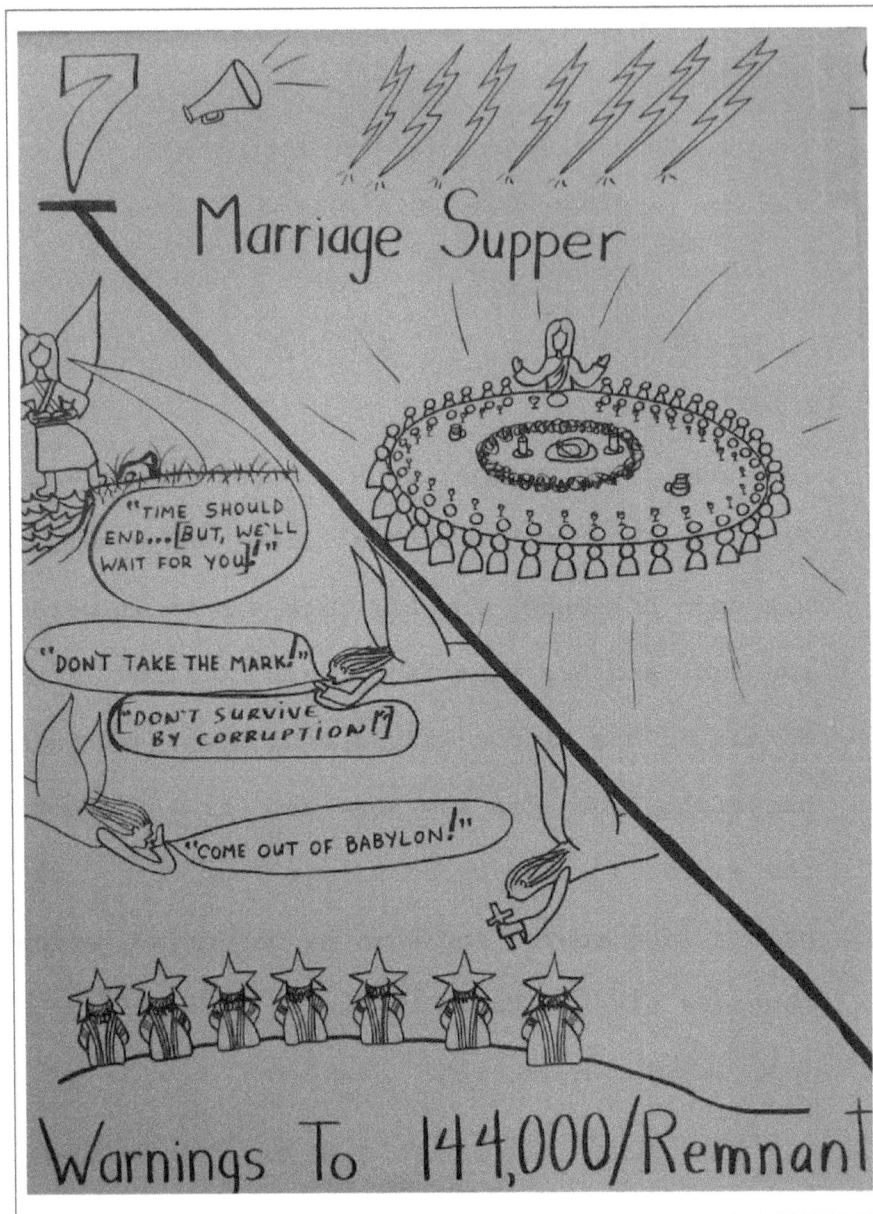

(Fig. 17 -- Warnings & Marriage Supper)

'Authoritative' Antichrist-[Voice of Error/Evil]) will

be referred to as the 'Second Woe', and the Seven Last

Plagues will be referred to as the 'Third Woe'. **Rev 11:14-16** reads:

> "*(14)* **The second woe is past**—(i.e.; the Christian-Witnesses have been killed)*; and, behold, the third woe cometh quickly*—(i.e.; Seven Last Plagues of Wrath). *(15)* **And the seventh angel sounded** (Seventh Trump of Seventh Seal)*; and there were great voices in heaven, saying, the kingdoms of this world are become the kingdoms of our Lord, and of his Christ*—(i.e.; Jesus Christ has taken control of the Earth and all of its inhabitants*; and he shall reign for ever and ever. (16) And the four and twenty elders, which sat before God on their seats, fell upon their faces, and worshipped God,"* — (See; Fig. 17 [pg. 168])

Continuing across the Revelation Grid (from left to right)—(See; Fig. 3 [pg. 39]), we find that Chapter 14 also revisits the moment where God floods the Earth with angelic warnings after the Christian-Witnesses are killed/raised. Once again, the scripture clearly reflects God's unfailing love toward the Remnant of Israel. **Rev 14:6-7** reads:

"(6) And I saw another angel fly in the midst of heaven, having the everlasting Gospel (the Last Word) *to preach unto them that dwell on the earth, and to every nation, and kindred, and tongue, and people* (although, only the 144,000 will embrace it), *(7) Saying with a loud voice, Fear God, and give glory to him; for the hour of his judgment is come: and worship him that made heaven, and earth, and the sea, and the fountains of waters."* — (See; Fig. 17 [pg. 168])

Moving across the Revelation Grid (from left to right) again—(See; Fig. 3 [pg. 39]), we find that Chapter 18 focuses more on the condemnation of the Whore, at this point. **Rev 18:1-2** reads:

"(1) And after these things I saw another angel come down from heaven, having great power; and the Earth was lighted with his glory. (2) And he cried mightily with a strong voice, saying, Babylon the great-(the Antichrist-empowered/Authoritative Whore-soul of mankind; the 4th Kingdom of the world) *is fallen, is fallen*—(i.e.; has made her move against the Kingdom of God, and will now suffer her

punishment)*, and is become the habitation*-(home)
*of Devils, and the hold of every foul spirit, and
a cage*-(prison) *of every unclean and hateful bird*
(spirit)*."* — (See; Fig. 17 [pg. 168])

(**Rev 10:4-7** goes on, to say):

*"(4) And when the seven thunders had uttered
their voices, I was about to write* (their
prophecy)*: and I heard a voice from heaven saying
unto me, seal up those things which the seven
thunders uttered, and write them not. (5) And the
angel which I saw stand upon the sea and upon the
earth lifted up his hand to heaven, (6) And swore
by Him that lives forever and ever, who created
heaven, and the things that therein are, and the
earth, and the things that therein are, and the
sea, and the things which are therein, that there
should be time no longer* (however; God still has
to save one last [additional] Remnant of Israel —
so; time can't end here)*: (7) But in the days of
the voice of the seventh angel*-(Seventh Trump)*,
when he shall begin to sound* (Seven Thunders) *the
mystery of God should be finished* (will be

completed)**, as he hath declared to his servants the prophets.**" — (See; Fig. 17 [pg. 168])

As we see in the passages above, time 'should' cease when God finally separates that which is eternal from that which is temporary/time-based—(i.e.; when He reaps the end-time harvest). However; because the (Old Testament) rulers of Israel had blasphemed against the Holy Spirit of Truth (taking the Lost Sheep captive and greatly complicating their eventual redemption), God ended up having to (first) raise up an earlier harvest (the empowered Christian vessels), through whom He could draw out (and save) the Lost Sheep of Israel. For that reason, time cannot end after one (single) end-time harvest, as it 'should' have.

Moving across the Revelation Grid (from left to right)—(See; Fig. 3 [pg. 39]), we find that when Chapter 11 revisits this period of God's ministering angels flying through the Earth issuing His last warnings, Chapter 11 focusses on how the twenty four elders will praise God and His Son, in their great victory; **Rev 11:17-18** reads:

"*(17)* **Saying, We**-(the twenty four elders) **give you thanks, O Lord God Almighty, which are, and** *was, and are to come; because you have taken to you your great power, and hast reigned. (18) And the nations were angry, and your wrath is come, and the time of the* (still living) *dead, that they should be judged* (suffer their punishment), *and that you should give reward—*(i.e.; the Marriage Supper) *unto your servants the prophets, and to the saints, and them that fear your name, small and great; and should destroy* (the flesh of) *them which destroy the earth—*(i.e.; destroy the Whore souls of the Whore-Movement)." — (See; Fig. 17 [pg. 168])

Continuing across the Revelation Grid (from left to right)—(See; Fig. 3 [pg. 39]); Chapter 14 continues its focus on the Whore and the Beast during these angelic warnings, and it describes the end result of caving-in to the spirit of Error/Evil; **Rev 14:8-11** reads:

"(8) ***And there followed another angel, saying, Babylon-***(the Antichrist-empowered/Authoritative Whore-soul of mankind; the 4th Kingdom of the world) ***is fallen, is fallen—***(i.e.; made her move against the Kingdom of God, and will now suffer

her punishment)*, that great city, because she made all nations drink of the wine of the wrath of her fornication. (9) And the third angel followed them, saying with a loud voice, If any man worship-*(fear and obey) *the Beast-*(Legions of Error/Evil) *and his image-*(the Whores of Error/Evil)*, and receive his mark in his forehead, or in his hand* (being assessed as an offense against the Word of God or His people; assessed as part of the Beast [by their mindset or behavior])*, (10) The same shall drink of the wine of the wrath of God* (the Seven Last Plagues of Wrath)*, which is poured out without mixture into the cup of his indignation; and he shall be tormented with fire and brimstone in the presence of the holy angels, and in the presence of the Lamb. (11) And the smoke of their torment will ascend up for ever and ever: and they have no rest day nor night, who worship-*(fear and obey) *the Beast and his image, and whosoever received the mark of his name."* — (See; Fig. 17 [pg. 168]) Verses 9 and 10, above (as well as verse 4, below) state, that; only worshippers of Error/Evil

will drink of the wrath of the Seven Last Plagues.
This clearly indicates that the 144,000 (and, possibly
the [uncommitted] Lukewarms) will somehow 'not'
directly suffer from the Plagues. Continuing across
the Revelation Grid (from left to right)—(See; Fig. 3
[pg. 39]), we see that Chapter 18 continues to testify
of the longsuffering love of God and Jesus, toward
struggling mankind (so evident, in these ongoing
warnings to the Lost Sheep of Israel); **Rev 18:3-7**
reads:

> "*(3)* ***For all nations have drunk of the wine of
> the wrath of her***-(the Whore's) ***fornication, and
> the kings*** (authorities) ***of the earth have
> committed fornication with her, and the merchants
> of the earth are waxed rich through the abundance
> of her delicacies.*** *(4)* ***And I heard another voice
> from heaven*** (Jesus), ***saying, come out of her, my
> people***-(the 144,000/Remnant), ***that ye be not
> partakers of her sins, and that ye receive not of
> her plagues.*** *(5)* ***For her sins have reached unto
> heaven, and God hath remembered her iniquities.***
> *(6)* ***Reward her even as she rewarded you, and
> double unto her double according to her works: in***

*the cup which she hath filled fill to her double.
(7) How much she hath glorified herself, and
lived deliciously, so much torment and sorrow
give her: for she says in her heart, I sit a
queen, and am no widow* (not needing or longing
for her lost, first love; God)*, and shall see no
sorrow.*" — (See; Fig. 17 [pg. 168])

In the verses above, we see that although God has
sealed the 144,000 (to have their eyes and hearts
opened to Jesus), their salvation is still completely
dependent upon their own choice to behave obediently
toward God and man once their eyes are opened. Moving
down and across the Revelation Grid, Chapter 14 offers
a quick glimpse into what it is (exactly) that will
strengthen (and spare) the 144,000/Remnant as the
world struggles through the Tribulations-Period. **Rev
14:12-13** reads:

"*(12) Here* (in the everlasting Gospel) *is the
patience* (Holy Spirit) *of the* (new) *saints* (the
144,000)*: here are they that keep the
commandments of God* (the First Word; the Old
Testament)*, and the faith of Jesus* (the Last
Word; the New Testament). *(13) And I heard a*

voice from heaven saying unto me, Write, blessed are the dead which die in the Lord from henceforth—(i.e.; blessed are the 144,000/Remnant who will 'die in the Lord' when they are immortalized [at the end of the Tribulations-Period]): *Yea, says the Spirit, that they may rest from their labors; and their works do follow them."* — (See; Fig. 17 [pg. 168])

Again; during this relatively short interval of warnings and reflection (between the harvest of the Christian-Witnesses and the beginning of the Seven Last Plagues of Wrath) God issues His final warning, which basically says; "Do not become willing to offend the Word of God or His Kingdom, to survive". In the verses below, God lets the 144,000/Remnant know (in no uncertain terms) that the end is going to be sweet, but the means will not be. **Rev 10:8-11** reads:

"(8) And the voice which I heard from heaven spake unto me again, and said, Go and take the little book which is open in the hand of the angel which stands upon the sea and upon the earth. (9) And I went unto the angel, and said unto him, Give me the little book. And he said

unto me, Take it, and eat it up; and it shall make your belly bitter, but it shall be in your mouth sweet as honey. (10) *And I took the little book out of the angel's hand, and ate it up; and it was in my mouth sweet as honey: and as soon as I had eaten it, my belly was bitter.* (11) *And he said unto me, Thou*-(John, son of Zebedee) *must prophecy again* (what was written in the little book) *before many peoples, and nations, and tongues, and kings."* — (See; Fig. 17 [pg. 168])

Interesting is the delicate balance of the Lukewarm-soul throughout all the generations of time; navigating between the goodness/mercy of Christianized mankind and the evil/convenience of Whore mankind. One thing the Lukewarms have always appreciated about the Whore is that the Whore has no problem performing the corruption that accomplishes the end-goals the Lukewarms sometimes share with them. The Lukewarms are rarely willing to outwardly be the 'bad guy'; however, they have little reservation about looking the other way when the Whore's actions will also benefit them. Their character is made very clear when they celebrate the Whore's annihilation of the Christian-Witnesses at the end of the Sorrows-Period (which frees the Lukewarms from the 'oppression' of Christian-standards).

Unfortunately for the Lukewarm kings, immediately after they celebrate the destruction of the Christian-Witnesses, they find themselves completely oppressed by Error/Evil and quickly resolve to destroy the Whore, too. This they do, thinking the Earth will finally become theirs (a Lukewarm-Reign). What they don't know, is that immediately after they destroy the Whore, God will immortalize the 144,000 new Christians and put them in charge, on Earth; leaving the Lukewarms right back at square one. For the next 1,000 years, the Lukewarms will be completely oppressed by Christian standards, and their loss of the Whore's 'balancing'-influence will impact them profoundly (just as the loss of the Christian-Witnesses had [unexpectedly] impacted them profoundly). Moving down and across the Revelation Grid (from left to right)—(See; Fig. 3 [pg. 39]), we see that Chapter 18 begins to describe how (and why) the Lukewarm-souls are going to miss the great Whore when she is destroyed. **Rev 18:8-13** goes on, to say:

*"(8) **Therefore shall her-**(the Whore) **plagues come in one day, death, and mourning, and famine; and she shall be utterly burned with fire: for strong is the Lord God who judges her.** (9) **And the** (Lukewarm) **kings of the earth, who have committed fornication and lived deliciously with her, shall bewail her, and lament for her, when they shall see the smoke of her burning,** (10) **standing afar off for the fear of her torment, saying, Alas, alas, that great city Babylon-**(the Antichrist-empowered/Authoritative Whore-soul of mankind; the 4th Kingdom of the world), **that mighty city! for in one hour is your judgment come.** (11) **And the** (Lukewarm) **merchants of the earth shall weep and mourn over her; for no man buys their merchandise any more.** (12) **The merchandise of gold, and silver, and precious stones, and of pearls, and fine linen, and purple, and silk, and scarlet, and all thyine wood, and all manner vessels of ivory, and all manner vessels of most precious wood, and of brass, and iron, and marble,** (13) **And cinnamon, and odors, and ointments, and frankincense, and wine, and oil,***

and fine flour, and wheat, and Beasts, and sheep, and horses, and chariots, and slaves, and souls of men." — (See; Fig. 17 [pg. 168])

(**Rev 18:14-19** goes on, to say):

"(14) And the fruits that your (Lukewarm) *soul lusted after are departed from you, and all things which were dainty and goodly are departed from you, and you shall find them no more at all. (15) The* (Lukewarm) *merchants of these things, which were made rich by her, shall stand afar off for the fear of her torment, weeping and wailing, (16) And saying, Alas, alas, that great city, that was clothed in fine linen, and purple, and scarlet, and decked with gold, and precious stones, and pearls! (17) For in one hour so great riches is come to naught. And every* (Lukewarm) *shipmaster, and all the company in ships, and sailors, and as many as trade by sea, stood afar off, (18) And cried when they saw the smoke of her burning, saying, What city is like unto this great city! (19) And they cast dust on their heads, and cried, weeping and wailing, saying, Alas, alas, that great city, wherein were made*

rich all that had ships in the sea by reason of her costliness! for in one hour is she made desolate." — (See; Fig. 17 [pg. 168])

Bear in mind that the Whore has not yet 'been' destroyed (at this point in the Revelation); the verses above and below are only revealing how the Lukewarms-(Self-worshippers; Magog) are 'going' to miss the Whore, when she is finally destroyed. **Rev 18:20-24** goes on, to say:

"(20) Rejoice over her, you heaven, and ye holy apostles and prophets; for God hath avenged you on her. (21) And a mighty angel took up a stone like a great millstone, and cast it into the sea, saying, Thus with violence shall that great city Babylon-(the empowered/ Authoritative Whore-soul of mankind; the 4th Kingdom of the world) *be thrown down, and shall be found no more at all. (22) And the voice of harpers, and musicians, and of pipers, and trumpeters, shall be heard no more at all in you*—(i.e.; within the 4th Kingdom; Babylon)*; and no craftsman, of whatsoever craft he be, shall be found any more in you; and the sound of a millstone shall be heard no more at*

all in you; (23) *And the light of a candle shall shine no more at all in you; and the voice of the Bridegroom-*(Jesus) *and of the Bride-*(collective-soul of Godly mankind) *shall be heard no more at all in you—*(i.e.; they will be eternally separated from the 4th Kingdom)*: for your merchants were the great men of the earth; for by your sorceries were all nations deceived.* (24) *And in her was found the blood of prophets, and of saints, and of all that were slain upon the earth."* — (See; Fig. 17 [pg. 168])

And then, just as carefully and vibrantly as the angel has depicted the overwhelming loss that will be experienced on Earth (among the Lukewarms) when the Whore is destroyed — he now begins to regale us with a beautiful description of the overwhelming joy that will be taking place on the Sea of Glass during that same moment in time (the judgement of the [harvested] 'just'); as the immortalized Kingdom of God prepares to attend the Marriage Supper of the Lamb. **Rev 19:1-6** reads:

"(1) And after these things I heard a great voice of much people in heaven (collective-soul of

[resurrected] Godly mankind), *saying, Alleluia;*

Salvation, and glory, and honor, and power, unto

the Lord our God. (2) For true and righteous are

his judgments: for he hath judged the great Whore

('set in motion' the Seventh Trump events), *which*

did corrupt the earth with her fornication, and

hath avenged the blood of his servants at her

hand. (3) And again they said, Alleluia. And her

smoke rose up for ever and ever. (4) And the four

and twenty elders and the four Beasts fell down

and worshipped God that sat on the throne,

saying, Amen; Alleluia. (5) And a voice came out

of the throne, saying, praise our God, all ye his

servants, and ye that fear him, both small and

great. (6) And I heard as it were the voice of a

great multitude, and as the voice of many waters,

and as the voice of mighty thunderings, saying,

Alleluia: for the Lord God omnipotent reigns." —

(See; Fig. 17 [pg. 168])

(**Rev 19:7-10** goes on, to say):

"*(7) Let us be glad and rejoice, and give honor*

to him: for the marriage of the lamb is come, and

his wife-(collective-soul of [resurrected] Godly

mankind) *hath made herself ready. (8) And to her was granted that she should be arrayed in fine linen, clean and white: for the fine linen* (her White Robe) *is the righteousness of saints. (9) And he says unto me, Write, blessed are they which are called unto the marriage supper of the Lamb. And he says unto me, These are the True sayings of God. (10) And I fell at his feet to worship him. And he said unto me, See you do it not: I am your fellowservant, and of your brethren that have the testimony of Jesus* (this speaker is a resurrected soul, speaking from the throne of God): *worship God: for the testimony of Jesus is the spirit of prophecy."* — (See; Fig. 17 [pg. 168])

The above verses clearly reveal that the Marriage Supper occurs immediately after the Christian-Witnesses/Two-Witnesses are killed and raised (at the end of the 3.5-year Sorrows-Period), whereas, the 144,000 will not even be 'immortalized' until the end of the 3.5-year Tribulations-Period. Next, we will learn that immediately after the Marriage Supper, the Temple in Heaven opens and Jesus comes to Earth with his army (Legions of Heavenly angels) to initiate the Seven Last Plagues of Wrath (i.e.; the Second Coming); at the end of which, he will immortalize the 144,000/Remnant of Israel.

We can clearly discern from these verses that the 'Second Coming' does not occur during the harvest of the Christian-Witnesses (wherein, Jesus simply calls the harvest up into Heaven). Rather; the Second Coming occurs when Jesus returns with his army-(Legions of Heavenly angels) after the Marriage Supper (to initiate the 3.5-year Tribulations-Period-[Seven Last Plagues of Wrath]). Consider the following verses, which add subtle nuances to the Marriage Supper of the Lamb:

> *(Ref: Matt 25:1-13)—"(1) Then shall the Kingdom of Heaven be likened unto ten virgins, which took their lamps, and went forth to meet the Bridegroom. (2) And five of them were wise-* (possessing anointed Seed of Holy Ghost, plus; Old and New Testament Words/amendments]), *and five were foolish-* (lacking anointed Seed of Holy Ghost and lacking New Testament Word/amendment). *(3) They that were foolish took their lamps* (Old

Testament Word)*, and took no oil* (anointed Seed of Holy Ghost) *with them: (4) But the wise took oil* (anointed Seed of Holy Ghost) *in their vessels with their lamps* (Old and New Testament Words/amendments). *(5) While the Bridegroom tarried, they all slumbered and slept. (6) And at midnight there was a cry made, behold, the Bridegroom cometh; go ye out to meet him. (7) Then all those virgins arose, and trimmed their lamps* (tended the Word). *(8) And the foolish said unto the wise* (realizing they lacked light; having no oil)*, Give us of your oil; for our lamps are gone out* (the light of their garment had gone dim). *(9) But the wise answered, saying, Not so; lest there be not enough for us and you: but go ye rather to them that sell, and* (trade everything, to) *buy for yourselves—*(i.e.; acquire it at your own cost, so you will have it when Jesus returns again after the Marriage Supper). *(10) And while they went* (to trade everything) *to buy, the Bridegroom came; and they that were ready* (the Christianized Witnesses) *went in with him to the marriage* (were harvested): *and the* *door was shut. (11) Afterward came also the other virgins* (the 'awakened' 144,000), *saying, Lord, Lord, open to us* (we now recognize and accept you). *(12) But he answered and said, Verily I say unto you, I-*(Jesus) *know you not—*(i.e.; Jesus has not [yet] lived 'through' their hearts. The 144,000 will have to wait until they come to 'know' Jesus [and Jesus comes to 'know' them]; through the Tribulations-Period). *(13) Watch therefore, for ye know neither the day nor the hour wherein the Son of man cometh."*

And...

(Ref: Luke 12:35-40)—"*(35) Let your loins be girded about, and your lights burning* (with Holy Ghost); *(36) And ye yourselves-*(144,000/Remnant) *like unto men that wait for their Lord, when he will return from the wedding-*(Marriage Supper); *that when he comes-*(Second Coming) *and knocks, they may open unto him immediately. (37) Blessed are those servants, whom the lord when he cometh shall find watching: verily I say unto you, that he* (that faithful servant) *shall gird himself, and make them* (the hungry sheep) *to sit down to meat, and will come forth and serve them*—(i.e.; the faithful servant will be strengthening his brethren, when Jesus comes). *(38) And if he-* (Jesus) *shall come in the second watch* (the Christian harvest)*, or come in the third watch* (the 144,000/Remnant harvest)*, and find them so* (serving the Kingdom)*, blessed are those servants. (39) And this know, that if the goodman of the house had known what hour the thief would come, he would have watched, and not have suffered his house to be broken through. (40) Be ye therefore ready also: for the Son of man cometh at an hour when ye think not.*"

Notice (at the beginning of the above verses) that the angel is speaking to souls who have 'yet' to be harvested — advising them to wait for the Lord who will 'return from' the Marriage Supper. This verse clearly distinguishes between the already harvested Christian Church (who celebrates the Marriage Supper 'with' Jesus) and the 144,000/Remnant (that have not yet been harvested, by this point).

CHAPTER 7 — THE TRIBULATIONS-PERIOD; SEVEN LAST PLAGUES

The period between the harvest of the Christian-Witnesses and the beginning of the Tribulations-Period-(Seven Last Plagues of Wrath) is very brief; just long enough for the angels to issue God's warnings on Earth while the Bride celebrates the Marriage Supper with Jesus, in Heaven. At the conclusion of the Marriage Supper, the Temple in Heaven will be opened and Jesus will muster his army (Legions of Heavenly angels) to fall hard upon the Earth and its inhabitants. **Rev 11:19** reads:

"*(19)* **And the Temple of God was opened in heaven, and there was seen in his temple the ark of his testament: and there were lightnings, and voices,** *and thunderings, and an earthquake, and great hail."* — (See; Fig. 18 [pg. 193])

Moving across the Revelation Grid (from left to right)—(See; Fig. 3 [pg. 39]), we find that when Chapter 14 revisits the opening of the Temple, it describes the command from Heaven that initiates the Seven Last Plagues of Wrath-(Tribulations-Period). **Rev 14:17-18** reads:

"(17) **And another angel came out of the Temple which is in heaven, he also having a sharp sickle.** *(18)* **And another angel came out from the altar, which had power over fire; and cried with a loud cry to him that had the sharp sickle, saying, Thrust in your sharp sickle, and gather the clusters of the vine of the Earth; for her grapes are fully ripe**—(i.e.; setting his hand for a second end-time harvest; preparing the stage for that harvest)." — (See; Fig. 18 [pg. 193])

Continuing across the Revelation Grid (from left to right)—(See; Fig. 3 [pg. 39]), we find that when Chapter 19 revisits the opening of the Temple, it focuses solely on the person of Jesus, Himself; as he

(Fig. 18 -- Second Coming; Jesus Returns with Army)

prepares to leave Heaven with his army. **Rev 19:11-13** reads:

"(11) And I saw Heaven opened, and behold a white horse; and he that sat upon him (Jesus) *was called Faithful and True, and in righteousness he doth judge and make war. (12) His eyes were as a flame of fire, and on his head were many crowns; and he had a name written, that no man knew, but he himself. (13) And he was clothed with a vesture dipped in blood: and his name is called The Word of God* (First and Last Words; Old and New Testaments)." — (See; Fig. 18 [pg. 193])

Moving down and across the Revelation Grid (from left to right)—(See; Fig. 3 [pg. 39]), we find that Chapter 14 goes on to describe what Israel's redemption (by judgement) will look like as the Seven Last Plagues of Wrath are unleashed upon the Earth.

Rev 14:19-20 & 15:1 reads:

"(19) And the (other) *angel thrust in his sickle into the earth, and gathered the vine of the earth*—(i.e.; collected the 144,000/Remnant of Israel), *and cast it into the great winepress of the wrath of God*—(i.e.; into the Tribulations-Period). *(20) And the winepress was trodden without the city*—(i.e.; trodden 'outside of' the

Kingdom/Remnant)*, and blood came out of the winepress, even unto the horse bridles, by the space of a thousand and six hundred furlongs. (Ch. 15) (1) And I saw another sign in heaven, great and marvelous, seven angels having the seven last plagues; for in them is filled up the wrath of God."* — (See; Fig. 18 [pg. 193])

Moving across the Revelation Grid (from left to right)—(See; Fig. 3 [pg. 39]); when Chapter 15 revisits the initiation of the Seven Last Plagues of Wrath, we see a description of the Seven Angels (who embody the Plagues) being given Seven Vials of Wrath; **Rev 15:5-8** reads:

"*(5) And after that I looked, and, behold, the Temple of the tabernacle of the testimony in heaven was opened. (6) And the seven angels came out of the Temple, having the seven plagues, clothed in pure and white linen, and having their breasts girded with golden girdles. (7) And one of the four Beasts gave unto the seven angels seven golden vials full of the wrath of God, who lives for ever and ever. (8) And the temple was filled with smoke from the glory of God, and from his power; and no man* (not one, single harvested child of God) *was able to enter into the Temple, till* (after) *the Seven Plagues of the seven angels were fulfilled."* — (See; Fig. 18 [pg. 193])

According to the passage above, the seven angels apparently embody the Seven Plagues — and, the Seven Vials appear to be a measure of God's wrath (to be applied to their distribution). When the Early-Saints were raised into Heaven (2,000+ years ago), their presence was restricted to the Sea of Glass (at the foot of the altar of God). And when the harvested Christian-Witnesses join them, they too will be restricted to the Sea of Glass (and, all of them will be unable to enter into the Temple [in Heaven] until all seven of the Plagues of Wrath have been fulfilled and the 144,000/Remnant are added to their ranks). But for now, all of the harvested Christian-Witnesses and resurrected Saints will begin ministering to the still mortal 144,000/Remnant (directly from the Sea of Glass), and will do so for the duration of the 3.5-year Tribulations-Period (and presumably for the entire duration of the 1,000-Year-Reign). Continuing across the Revelation Grid (from left to right)—(See; Fig. 3 [pg. 39]), **Rev 19:14-16** reads:

"*(14)* ***And the armies which were in heaven*** (God's Legions of angels) ***followed him***-(Jesus) ***upon white horses, clothed in fine linen, white and clean.*** *(15)* ***And out of his mouth goes a sharp sword*** (his Word; two-edged sword)***, that with it he should smite the nations: and he shall rule them with a rod of iron: and he treads the winepress of the fierceness and wrath of Almighty God*** (he governs the angels dispensing the Seven Last Plagues of Wrath). *(16)* ***And he hath on his vesture and on his thigh a name written, King of Kings, and Lord of Lords.***" — (See; Fig. 18 [pg. 193])

Consider the following prophetic verses, which provide even more details about the Second Coming of Jesus:

(Ref: Isa 13:3-6)—"*(3) I have commanded my sanctified ones*—(i.e.; I have instructed the resurrected Christians and Saints to minister to the [mortal] 144,000/Remnant), *I have also called my mighty ones* (Legions of Heavenly angels; his

army) *for mine anger, even them that rejoice in my highness. (4) The noise of a multitude in the mountains, like as of a great people; a tumultuous noise of the kingdoms of nations gathered together: The Lord of hosts musters the host of the battle. (5) They come from a far country, from the end of Heaven, even the Lord, and the weapons of his indignation, to destroy the whole land. (6) Howl ye; for the day of the Lord is at hand* (the Second Coming)*; it shall come as a destruction from the Almighty."*

And...

(Ref: Mic 1:3-4)—"(3) For, behold, the Lord cometh forth out of his place, and will come down (from the Temple in Heaven)*, and tread upon the high places of the earth. (4) And the mountains shall be molten under him, and the valleys shall be cleft, as wax before the fire, and as the waters that are poured down a steep place."*

And...

(Ref: Zech 14:3-10)—"(3) Then shall the Lord go forth, and fight against those nations, as when he fought in the day of battle. (4) and his feet

shall stand in that day upon the mount of Olives,

which is before Jerusalem on the east, and the

mount of Olives shall cleave in the midst thereof

toward the east and toward the west, and there

shall be a very great valley....And ye-(Israel)

shall flee to the valley of the mountains...and

the Lord my God shall come, and all the saints

with you (ministering to you) *....And the Lord*

shall be king over all the earth: in that day

shall there be one Lord, and his name one. (10)

All the land shall be turned as a plain...unto

the king's winepresses."

And...

(Ref: Matt 24:21-44 [& Mark 13:18-37 & Luke

21:25-36])—"(21) For then shall be great

tribulation, such as was not since the beginning

of the world to this time, no, nor ever shall be.

(And there shall be [beginning] *signs in the sun,*

and in the moon, and in the stars—[i.e.; the

'Beginning of Sorrows']; *and upon the earth*

distress of nations, with perplexity; the sea and

the waves roaring; Men's hearts failing them for

fear, and for looking after those things which

are coming on the earth: for the powers of heaven shall be shaken [Luke 21:25-26].) (22) And except those days (Sorrows/Tribulations-Period) *should be shortened* (as they will, for the Christian-Witnesses)*, there should no flesh be saved: but for the elect's sake those days* (Sorrows/Tribulations-Period) *shall be shortened* (to Sorrows-Period). *(23) Then* (during the Sorrows-Period) *if any man shall say unto you, Lo, here is Christ, or there* (the Second Coming; Tribulations-Period)*...believe it not. (For false Christs and false prophets shall rise, and shall shew signs and wonders, to seduce, if it were possible, even the elect [Mark 13:22].) (27) For as the lightning cometh out of the east, and shines even unto the west; so shall also the* (second) *coming of the Son of man be*—(i.e.; every man will see it, for himself). *(28) For wheresoever the carcass is* (the dead bodies of the Christian-Witnesses, as the Sorrows-Period comes to a close)*, there will the eagles be gathered together* (angels of God, eating the flesh). *(29) Immediately after the tribulation of* *those days* (after the 3.5-year Sorrows-Period) *shall the sun be darkened, and the moon shall not give her light, and the stars shall fall from heaven* (Jesus and his angels, descending on the Earth)*, and the powers of the heavens shall be shaken: (30)And then shall appear the sign of the Son of man in heaven* (Jesus, with his army)*: and then shall all the tribes of the earth mourn, and they shall see the son of man coming in the clouds of heaven with power and great glory. (31) And he shall send his angels with a great sound of a trumpet, and they shall gather together his elect from the four winds, from one end of heaven to the other. (32) Now learn a parable of the fig tree; When his branch is yet tender, and puts forth leaves, ye know that summer is nigh: (33) So likewise ye, when ye shall see all these things* (beginning with the signs of the Sorrows-Period)*, know that it is near, even at the doors...in the days that were before the flood they were eating and drinking, marrying and giving in marriage, until the day that Noah entered into the ark, (39) And knew not until the* *flood came, and took them all away; so shall also the* (Second) *coming of the Son of Man be—*(i.e.; the warning signs will be provided, but many will not believe or prepare). *(40) Then shall two* (of Israel) *be in the field; the one shall be taken, and the other left. (41) Two women* (of Israel) *shall be grinding at the mill; the one shall be taken, and the other left.* (Heaven and earth shall pass away: but my Words shall not pass away. But of that day and that hour knows no man, no, not the angels which are in heaven, neither the Son, but the Father [Mark 13:31-32].) *(42) Watch therefore: for ye know not what hour your Lord doth come. (43) But know this, that if the goodman of the house had known in what watch the thief would come, he would have watched, and would not have suffered his house to be broken up.* (For the Son of man is as a man taking a far journey, who left his house, and gave authority to his servants, and to every man his work, and commanded the porter to watch [Mark 13:34].) (Verily I say unto you, This generation shall not pass away, till all be fulfilled. Heaven and *earth* (as we know it) *shall pass away: but my Words shall not pass away. And take heed to yourselves, lest at any time your hearts be overcharged with surfeiting, and drunkenness, and cares of this life, and so that day come upon you unawares. For as a snare shall it come on all them that dwell on the face of the whole earth. Watch ye therefore, and pray always, that ye may be accounted worthy to escape all these things that shall come to pass* (by becoming Christianized 'before' the harvest of the Christian-Witnesses—[i.e.; in the 'summer', rather than in the 'winter'])*, and to stand before the Son of man [Luke 21:32-36]). (44) Therefore be ye also ready: for in such an hour as ye think not the Son of man cometh."*

Moving down the Revelation Grid—(See; Fig. 3 [pg. 39]), we see that Chapter 16 begins to unfold the devastation of the Seven Last Plagues of Wrath, one vial at a time. (The distribution of these vials is the Third Woe promised to mankind in Rev 9:12). **Rev 16:1-2** reads:

(First Vial of the Seven Plagues of Wrath)—"*(1)* *And I heard a great voice out of the temple saying to the seven angels, Go your ways, and pour out the vials of the wrath of God upon the earth.* *(2)* *And the first* (angel) *went, and poured out his vial upon the earth; and there fell a noisome and grievous sore upon the men which had the mark of the Beast*—(i.e.; upon those assessed as an offense against the Word of God or His people; assessed as part of the Beast [by their mindset or behavior])*, and upon them which worshipped*-(feared and obeyed) *his image*-(the Whores of Error/Evil)." — (See; Fig. 19 [pg. 205])

The above verse suggests that this grievous sore will only affect ungodly mankind (the Whore, and possibly the Lukewarm), but not the 144,000/Remnant. **Rev 16:3** goes on, to say:

(Second Vial of the Seven Plagues of Wrath)—"*(3)* *And the second angel poured out his vial upon the sea; and it became as the blood of a dead man: and every living soul*-(every life-form that moves

(Fig. 19 -- Tribulations-Period; First Five Plagues)

under its own power/will) **died in the sea."** —

(See; Fig. 19 [pg. 205])

In Genesis, we learn that Adam 'became a living soul' when God breathed into his crafted, lifeless body the Breath of Life-(will/soul), but Adam's 'breath of life' also happened to include the Seed of the Holy Spirit. In other words; Adam's inanimate body became enlivened upon receipt of the spiritual soul/will-(life) — as did the bodies of every other living creature [see; Gen 1:21, Job 12:10] — but it wasn't Adam's soul-(will) that made him the 'image of God'; it was his heart. A 'soul' is simply a lifeform that can move under its own power/will, by design.

Earlier (during the Second Trump of the Seventh Seal [in the Sorrows-Period]) we saw all 'anointed'-(3rd Part, only)-ocean life being destroyed, and the oceans being contaminated. What we are now seeing (in Rev 16:3 [in Tribulations-Period]), is the remainder of all ocean life being destroyed (during the Second Vial/Plague of the Seventh Trump [of the Seventh Seal]). **Rev 16:4-7** goes on, to say:

(Third Vial of the Seven Plagues of Wrath)—"*(4)*

And the third angel poured out his vial upon the rivers and fountains of waters; and they became blood. *(5)* ***And I heard the angel of the waters***

say, you are righteous, O Lord, which art, and was, and shall be, because you have judged thus. (6) For they have shed the blood of saints and prophets, and you have given them blood to drink; for they are worthy. (7) And I heard another out of the altar say, Even so, Lord God Almighty, true and righteous are your judgments." — (See; Fig. 19 [pg. 205]).

Earlier (during the Third Trump of the Seventh Seal [in Sorrows-Period]) we saw all 'anointed'-(3rd Part, only)-Rivers and fountains tainted by Wormwood (which caused many men to die). What we are now seeing (in the verse above [in Tribulations-Period]), is that 'all' of these natural drinking-water sources have now become completely contaminated; probably by death and decay (in this Third Vial/Plague of the Seventh Trump [of the Seventh Seal]). **Rev 16:8-9** goes on, to say:

(Fourth Vial of the Seven Plagues of Wrath)—"*(8) And the fourth angel poured out his vial upon the sun; and power was given unto him* (the fourth angel) *to scorch men with fire. (9) And men were scorched with great heat, and blasphemed the name of God, which hath power over these plagues: and they repented not to give him glory."* — (See; Fig. 19 [pg. 205]).

Earlier (during the Fourth Trump of the Seventh Seal [in Sorrows-Period]) we saw the 'anointed'-(3ʳᵈ Part, only)-sun, moon and stars darkened (so that their light-emission was dimmed). What we are now seeing (in the verse above [in Tribulations-Period]), is that; despite its dimmed-light, the sun's heat will nevertheless become intensified, somehow (in this Fourth Vial/Plague of the Seventh Trump [of the Seventh Seal]); perhaps by moving nearer to the Earth, or, perhaps if it superheats [as stars do, just before they explode]? **Rev 16:10-11** goes on, to say:

(Fifth Vial of the Seven Plagues of Wrath)—"*(10)* **And the fifth angel poured out his vial upon the seat of the Beast; and his kingdom was full of darkness; and they gnawed their tongues for pain,** *(11)* **And blasphemed the God of heaven because of their pains and their sores, and repented not of their deeds."** — (See; Fig. 19 [pg. 205])

Earlier (during the Fifth Trump of the Seventh Seal [in Sorrows-Period]) we saw an angel descend to the Earth to open the Bottomless Pit (unleashing a great [evil] smoke, which began to fill the Earth with hatred and violence [through ungodly mankind]). What we are now seeing (in the verse above [in Tribulations-Period]), is the degree to which ungodly mankind will become engorged with that darkness and rage (in this Fifth Vial/Plague of the Seventh Trump [of the Seventh Seal]), just as the Battle-of-Armageddon is about to commence. Consider the following prophetic (Old Testament) verse, regarding the darkness of this time:

> *(Ref: Isa 13:9-11)—"(9) Behold, the day of the Lord cometh, cruel both with wrath and fierce anger, to lay the land desolate: and he shall destroy the sinners thereof out of it. (10) For the stars of heaven and the constellations thereof shall not give their* (anointed?) *light: the sun shall be darkened in his going forth, and the moon shall not cause her light to shine. (11) And I will punish the world for their Evil, and the wicked for their iniquity; and I will cause the arrogancy of the proud to cease, and will lay low the haughtiness of the terrible."*

When the 3.5-year Tribulations-Period-(Seven Last Plagues of Wrath) is nearing its end, the Lord will muster his army (Legions of heavenly angels) together for the great Battle of Armageddon. At Armageddon, he will destroy the 'flesh' of every Whore-soul, wherein; their will-(spiritual-aspect of soul) will fall into sleep, and their husband-spirit-(Legion/Beast [with his Antichrist Voice) will be cast into the Lake of Fire. At this time, the Devil-(Father of Error/Evil) will be imprisoned in the Bottomless Pit (withheld from the face of the Earth) for the duration of the upcoming 1,000-Year-Reign. (The Voice of Error/Evil will not be able to seduce the Lukewarm-mindset or the 144,000 for the next 1,000 years.)

Returning to the onset of the Battle of Armageddon; **Rev 16:12-13** reads:

(Sixth Vial of the Seven Plagues of Wrath)—"*(12)* ***And the sixth angel poured out his vial upon the great river Euphrates; and the water thereof was dried up, that the way of the kings of the east might be prepared.*** *(13)* ***And I saw three unclean spirits***-(the Antichrist voice; calling troops to arms) ***like frogs come out of the mouth of the***

Dragon-(Father of Error/Evil)*, and out of the mouth of the Beast*-(Legions of Error/Evil)*, and out of the mouth of the False Prophet*-(the Whore-souls and Lukewarm-souls)." — (See; Fig. 20 [pg. 212])

Earlier (during the Sixth Trump of the Seventh Seal [in Sorrows-Period]) we saw four angels released from the Euphrates River (who had been prepared in advance to destroy the 3rd Part of man [the anointed-Kingdom of the Sorrows-Period; the Christian-Witnesses]). What we are now seeing (in the verse above [in Tribulations-Period]), is that the Euphrates River is completely dried up (during the Sixth Vial/Plague of the Seventh Trump [of the Seventh Seal]), so that the invading armies have easy access to destroy the anointed-Kingdom of the Tribulations-Period (the 144,000/Remnant). At this point, the Antichrist Voice issues the command for his troops to fall into ranks.

In the verses above, we see the battle of Armageddon-(second Whore-Movement) beginning to unfold against the 144,000 (at the end of the Tribulations-Period) in strikingly similar fashion to the way the

(Fig. 20: 2nd Whore-Movement; Battle of Armageddon)

first Whore-Movement came against the Christian-

Witnesses (at the end of the Sorrows-Period); with

some pivotal activity originating in the Euphrates

River. Consider the following prophetic (Old Testament) verses, which offer some intricate details of the upcoming battle:

> *(Ref: Isa 11:11-16)*—"*(11) And it shall come to pass in that day, that the Lord shall set his hand again the second time*-(preparing the stage [again] for a second harvest-[at the Seventh Trump]) *to recover the Remnant of his people* (the 144,000), *which shall be left* (left behind from the Sixth Trump harvest [of Christian-Witnesses]), *from Assyria, and from Egypt, and from Pathros, and from Cush, and from Elam, and from Shinar, and from Hamath, and from the islands of the sea. (12) And He shall set up an ensign for the nations*—(i.e.; the confirmed 'Messiah'), *and shall assemble the outcasts of Israel, and gather together the dispersed of Judah from the four corners of the earth. (13) The envy also of Ephraim shall depart, and the adversaries of Judah shall be cut off: Ephraim shall not envy Judah, and Judah shall not vex Ephraim. (14) But they*-(all of Israel) *shall fly upon the shoulders of the philistines toward the*

west; they shall spoil them of the east together: they shall lay their hand upon Edom and Moab; and the children of Ammon shall obey them. (15) And the Lord shall utterly destroy the tongue of the Egyptian sea; and with His mighty wind shall he shake his hand over the river-(Euphrates), and shall smite it in the seven streams, and make men go over dryshod. (16) And there shall be an highway for the Remnant of his people (the 144,000 of Israel), *which shall be left, from Assyria; like as it was to Israel in the day that he came up out of the land of Egypt."*

And...

(Ref: Isa 27:12-13)—"(12) And it shall come to pass in that day, that the Lord shall beat off from the channel of the river unto the stream of Egypt, and ye shall be gathered one by one, O ye children of Israel. (13) And it shall come to pass in that day, that the great trumpet shall be blown, and they shall come which were ready to perish in the land of Assyria, and the outcasts in the land of Egypt, and shall worship the Lord in the holy mount at Jerusalem."

And...

(Ref: Ezek 29:3-5)—"(3) Speak, and say, Thus says the Lord God; behold, I am against you, Pharaoh (Whore) *king of Egypt, the great Dragon* (Devil; Satan) *that lies in the midst of his-*(Pharaoh's) *rivers, which hath said, my river is mine own, and I have made it for myself. (4) But I will put hooks in your jaws* (Devil)*, and I will cause the fish of your rivers to stick unto your scales* (being dead)*, and I will bring you up out of the midst of your rivers, and all the* (dead) *fish of your rivers shall stick unto your scales. (5) And I will leave you thrown into the wilderness, you and all the fish of your rivers: you shall fall upon the open fields; you shall not be brought together, nor gathered: I have given you for meat to the Beasts of the field and to the fowls of the heaven."*

Returning to the Revelation; Chapter 16 continues to elaborate on that initial muster-call issued by the Antichrist Voice. **Rev 16:14-16** reads:

"(14) **For they**-(the three unclean spirits/voices [call to arms] that came out of the mouth of the

Dragon, Beast and False Prophet) *are the spirits of Devils* (Voice of Error/Evil; Antichrist), *working miracles, which go forth unto the kings of the earth and of the whole world, to gather them* (call to arms) *to the battle of that great day of God Almighty* (the battle of Armageddon). *(15) Behold, I come as a thief. Blessed is he that watches, and keeps his garments*—(i.e.; continually embraces the light of the First and Last Words)*, lest he walk naked, and they see his shame* (this is a warning to the 144,000 of Israel. These cannot be overcome/deceived as long as they keep themselves immersed in the full Word of God; filled with Holy Spirit]). *(16) And he gathered them together into a place called in the Hebrew tongue Armageddon."* — (See; Fig. 20 [pg. 212])

Moving across the Revelation Grid (from left to right)—(See; Fig. 3 [pg. 39]); Chapter 19 revisits the Armageddon scenario and discusses how the fowls of Heaven will eat the flesh-(the physical-component) of the Whore-souls, when they are destroyed; **Rev 19:17-19** reads:

"(17) And I saw an angel standing in the sun; and he cried with a loud voice, saying to all the fowls that fly in the midst of Heaven, come and gather yourselves together unto the supper of the great God; (18) That ye may eat the flesh of kings, and the flesh of captains, and the flesh of mighty men—(i.e.; Whore mankind)*, and the flesh of horses, and of them that sit on them, and the flesh of ALL men, both free and bond, both small and great. (19) And I saw the Beast*—(Legions of Error/Evil)*, and the kings of the earth, and their armies, gathered together to make war against him that sat on the horse, and against his army."* — (See; Fig. 20 [pg. 212])

Consider what the following (Old Testament) prophets foretold, about the great battle of Armageddon:

(Ref: Psa 110:5-7)—*"(5) The Lord at your right hand shall strike through kings in the day of his wrath. (6) He shall judge among the heathen, he shall fill the places with the dead bodies; he shall wound the heads over many countries. (7) He shall drink of the brook in the way* (Euphrates): *therefore shall he lift up the head."*

And...

(Ref: Joel 3:11-14)-"(11) Assemble yourselves, and come, all ye heathen-(army of Evil/Error), *and gather yourselves together round about: thither cause your mighty ones-*(army; Legions of Heavenly angels) *to come down, o Lord. (12) Let the heathen be wakened, and come up to the valley of Jehoshaphat: for there will I sit to judge all the heathen round about. (13) Put ye in the sickle, for the harvest is ripe: come, get you down; for the press is full, the fats overflow; for their wickedness is great. (14) Multitudes, multitudes in the valley of decision: for the day of the Lord is near in the valley of decision."*

And...

(Ref: Dan 12:1)-"And at that time shall Michael stand up (an archangel-representation of the Lord), *the great prince which stands for the children of your people: and there shall be a time of trouble* (Tribulations-Period; Seven Last Plagues of Wrath), *such as never was since there*

was a nation even to that same time: and at that
time your people shall be delivered (the
144,000), *every one that shall be found written*
in the book."

What we haven't seen yet (but, soon will) is
that; although the Whore-souls believe that the ten
Lukewarm kings are suiting-up to charge 'with' them
(against the Kingdom of God [144,000]), God is
actually going to move in the minds of the ten
Lukewarm kings to work against the Whore, in this
battle; to utterly destroy the Whore.

Moving down and across the Revelation Grid—(See;
Fig. 3 [pg. 39]); Chapter 16 reveals the Seventh
(last) Vial that will be poured out onto mankind
(which results in the final destruction of the Whore).
Rev 16:17-18 reads:

(Seventh Vial of the Seven Plagues of Wrath)—
*"(17) **And the seventh angel poured out his vial***
into the air (to effect the 'swayable' climate of
the world [the Lukewarm-mindset])*; **and there came***
a great voice out of the temple of heaven, from
the throne, saying, it is done. (18) And there
were voices, and thunders, and lightenings; and

*there was a great earthquake, such as was not
since men were upon the earth, so mighty an
earthquake, and so great."*

The action of the Seventh angel, described above,
appears to be the moment where God moves the mind of
the Lukewarm kings to come up against the Whore (to
destroy her). Consider the following (upcoming) verse,
which will later reflect back on this moment in the
Revelation:

(Ref: Rev 17:16-17)—"(16) And the ten horns (the
ten Lukewarm kings) *which you saw upon the Beast-*
(Legions of Error/Evil), *these shall* (come to)
hate the Whore-(sold-out Evil mankind), *and shall
make her desolate and naked* (at Armageddon), *and*
(these ten Lukewarm kings) *shall eat her flesh,
and burn her with fire. (17) For God hath put it
in their hearts to fulfill His will* (to destroy
the committed bride of Legion), *and to agree, and
give their kingdom-*(their allegiance) *unto the
Beast* (who would be happy to kill all of mankind,
if God would let them), *until the Words of God
shall be fulfilled."*

Although the text of the 'Revelation of John' does not offer any additional details of the battle (itself), at this point in the scripture sequence, nevertheless; we can consider the following prophetic (Old Testament) verses that provide many of those details:

(Ref: Ezek 38:8 — 39:29)—"(8) After many days you shall be visited: in the latter years you- (Gog/Whore) *shall come into the land that is brought back from the sword, and* (the Remnant) *is gathered out of many people, against the mountains of Israel, which have been always waste: but it* (the Remnant of Israel) *is brought forth out of the nations, and they shall dwell safely all of them. (9) Thou-* (Gog/Whore; collective-soul of mankind that blasphemes Truth/Good; preferring the convenience of Error/Evil) *shall ascend and come like a storm, you shall be like a cloud to cover the land, thou, and all your bands, and many people with you. (10) Thus says the Lord God; It shall also come to pass, that at the same time shall things come into your mind, and you-* (Gog/Whore) *shall*

think an Evil thought: (11) *And you shall say, I will go up to the land of unwalled villages* (to attack the peaceful, devout of Israel; the 144,000/Remnant)*; I will go to them that are at rest, that dwell safely, all of them dwelling without walls, and having neither bars nor gates,* (12) *To take a spoil, and to take a prey; to turn thine hand upon the desolate places that are now inhabited, and upon the people that are gathered out of the nation....* (14) *Therefore, son of man, prophesy and say unto Gog-*(Whore)*, Thus says the Lord God; in that day when my people of Israel dwell safely, shall you not know it?* (15) *And you shall come from your place out of the north parts, thou, and many people with you, all of them riding upon horses, a great company, and a mighty army:* (16) *And you shall come up against my people of Israel* (surrounding them)*, as a cloud to cover the land; it shall be in the latter days* (the end-time)*, and I will bring you against my land, that the heathen may know me, when I shall be sanctified in you, O Gog, before their eyes....* (18) *And it shall come to pass at* *the same time when Gog-*(Whore) *shall come against the land of Israel* (surround them)*, says the Lord God, that my fury shall come up in my face....Surely in that day there shall be a great shaking in the land of Israel...and the mountains shall be thrown down, and the steep places shall fall, and every wall shall fall to the ground. (21) And I will call for a sword* (by authority of the Lukewarm kings) *against him* (Gog/Evil) *throughout all my mountains, says the Lord God: every* (warring) *man's sword shall be against his brother. (22) And I will plead against him* (through the Lukewarm armies) *with pestilence and with blood; and I will rain upon him, and upon his bands, and upon the many people that are with him, an overflowing rain, and great hailstones, fire, and brimstone. (23) Thus will I magnify myself, and sanctify myself; and I will be known in the eyes of many nations, and they shall know that I am the Lord. (Ch. 39) (1) Therefore, you son of man, prophesy against Gog-*(Whore)*, and say, Thus says the Lord God; behold, I am against you, O Gog-*(Whore)*, the chief prince of Meshech* *and Tubal: (2) and I will turn you back, and leave but the sixth part of you (of your entourage)*—(i.e.; He will leave alive of the ungodly those who are still only unaffiliated Lukewarms-[Magog; 6ᵗʰ Part])*, and will cause you to come up from the north parts, and will bring you upon the mountains of Israel: (3) And I will smite your bow out of your left hand, and will cause thine arrows to fall out of your right hand. (4) you-*(Whore; Gog) *shall fall upon the mountains of Israel* (at Armageddon)*, thou, and all your bands, and the people that is with you* (all of sold-out/Evil mankind)*: I will give you unto the ravenous birds of every sort, and to the Beasts of the field to be devoured. (5) you shall fall upon the open field: for I have spoken it, says the Lord God*—(See; Fig. 10[c] [pg. 225]).

(6) And I will (later) *send a* (devouring) *fire on Magog and among them that dwell carelessly* (without loyalty) *in the isles*—(i.e.; on all the Lukewarm-souls [at the end of the 1,000-Year-Reign])*: and they shall know that I am the Lord.... (8) Behold, it is come, and it is done,*

In The Lake of Fire	On The Sea of Glass	In The Grave	On The Earth
Beast & False Prophet (Antichrist)	Early Saints Christian Witnesses Buried Saints	Buried Sinners/Whore	Whore Mankind 'Devout' Jews (144,000) 'Lukewarm' Mankind

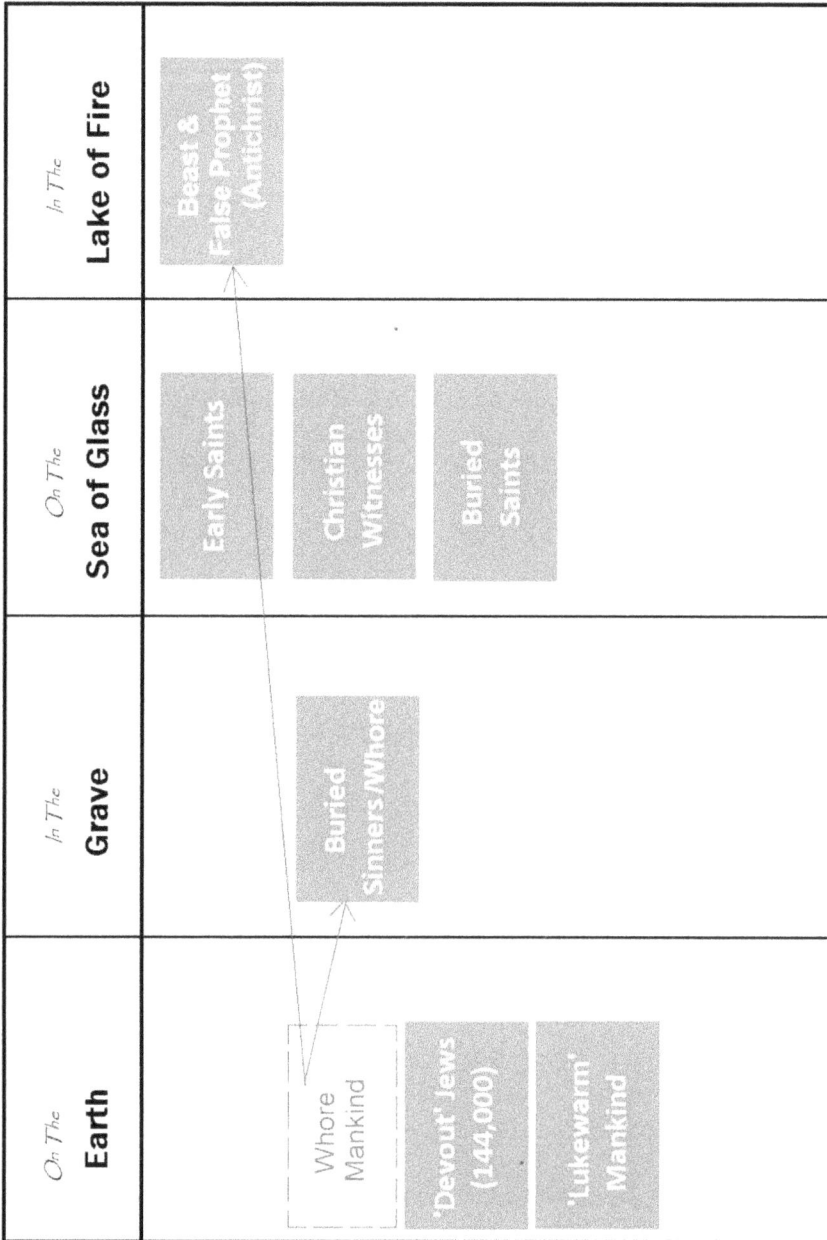

(Fig. 10c -- Whore-Mankind is Killed)

says the Lord God; this is the day whereof I have
spoken. (9) And they that dwell in the cities of
Israel shall go forth, and shall set on fire and
burn the weapons...and they shall burn them with

*fire seven years...they shall spoil those that
spoiled them, and rob those that robbed them,
says the Lord God. (11) And it shall come to pass
in that day, that I will give unto Gog-(Whore) a
place there of graves in Israel, the valley of
the passengers on the east of the sea...and they
shall call it The valley of Hamongog. (12) And
seven months shall the house of Israel be burying
of them, that they may cleanse the land.... (16)
And also the name of the city shall be Hamonah.
Thus shall they cleanse the land. (17) And, you
son of man, thus says the Lord God; speak unto
every feathered fowl, and to every Beast of the
field, assemble yourselves, and come; gather
yourselves on every side to my sacrifice that I
do sacrifice for you, even a great sacrifice upon
the mountains of Israel, that ye may eat flesh,
and drink blood...thus ye shall be filled at my
table with horses and chariots, with mighty men,
and with all men of war, says the Lord God. (21)
And I will set my glory-(Holy Zion) among the
heathen, and all the heathen shall see my
judgment that I have executed, and my hand that I*

have laid upon them. (22) So the house of Israel shall know that I am the Lord their God from that day and forward. (23) And the heathen shall know that the house of Israel went into captivity for their iniquity: because they trespassed against me, therefore hid I my face from them, and gave them into the hand of their enemies: so fell they all by the sword. (24) According to their uncleanness and according to their transgressions have I done unto them, and hid my face from them. (25) Therefore thus says the Lord God; now will I bring again the captivity of Jacob, and have mercy upon the whole house of Israel.... (26) After that they have borne their shame, and all their trespasses whereby they have trespassed against me.... (27) When I have brought them again from the people, and gathered them out of their enemies' lands, and am sanctified in them in the sight of many nations....I have gathered them unto their own land, and have left none of them any more there. (29) Neither will I hide my face any more from them: for I have poured out my spirit upon the house of Israel, says the Lord God."

Moving across the Revelation Grid (from left to right)—(See; Fig. 3 [pg. 39]); Chapter 19 reveals what will become of the Spirit of Error/Evil (which, indwells the Whore), once her flesh has been destroyed. **Rev 19:20** reads:

"(20) **And the Beast-**(collective-Legions of Error/Evil) **was taken** (overcome)*,* **and with him the False Prophet-**(Antichrist Voice; spoken, through the Whore-souls) **that wrought miracles before him-**(the Beast)*,* **with which he deceived them that had received the mark of the Beast—**(i.e.; the Voice with which he deceived those who were afterward assessed as an offense against the Word of God or His people; assessed as part of the Beast [by their mindset or behavior])*,* **and them that worshipped-**(feared and obeyed) **his image. These both-**(Beast-[Legions of Error/Evil] and False-Prophet/Antichrist-[Voice of Error/Evil]) **were cast alive into the lake of fire burning with brimstone."** — (See; Fig. 20 [pg. 212])

In the preceding verses, we once again see evidence that when the flesh of a Whore-soul is destroyed, their husband-spirit (Legion/Beast/Devil) is separated from that soul (in this case; cast into the Lake of Fire). Consider these (Old Testament) prophecies that discuss the Whore-Movements of the end-time, in general:

(Ref: Dan 7:19-28)—"(19) Then I would know the Truth of the fourth Beast—(i.e.; the 4th Kingdom; the full-force-Legion [of Error/Evil) inhabiting/driving the Whore-Movements of the end-time)*, which was diverse from all the others* (receiving free-reign to come against the Kingdom of God), *exceeding dreadful, whose teeth were of iron, and his nails of brass; which devoured, brake in pieces, and stamped the residue with his feet; (20) And of the ten horns* (the Lukewarm Kings) *that were in his head* —(i.e.; ten Lukewarm kings, who were of the same mind as the 4th Beast/Kingdom; rebelling against God's people), *and of the other* (horn) *which came up* (Authoritative Voice-of-Error/Antichrist)*, and before whom three* (horns/kings) *fell; even of*

that horn that had eyes, and a mouth that spake very great things, whose look was more stout than his fellows. (21) I beheld, and the same horn (Authoritative Voice-of-Error/Antichrist) *made war with the saints* (the Christian-Witnesses), *and prevailed against them; (22) Until the Ancient of days came* (Jesus, with his army), *and judgment* (authority) *was given to the saints of the most High; and the time came that the saints possessed the kingdom* (after Armageddon; for the 1,000-Year-Reign). *(23) Thus he said, the fourth Beast shall be the fourth* (world) *kingdom upon Earth, which shall be diverse* (different) *from all kingdoms* (having free reign to destroy Earth), *and shall* (function to) *devour the whole earth, and shall tread it down, and break it in pieces. (24) And the ten horns out of this* (4ᵗʰ) *kingdom are ten* (Lukewarm) *kings that shall arise* (in same mind as Whore-Kingdom; rebelling against God's people, through the Sorrows-Period): *and another* (king/'horn') *shall rise after them* (Authoritative/Full-strength Antichrist); *and he shall be diverse from the first, and he shall subdue three kings. (25) And he* (being 'Authoritative' Error/Evil) *shall speak great words against the most High, and shall wear out the saints of the most High* (the Kingdom of God), *and think to change times and laws: and they* (the Saints) *shall be given into his hand until a time and times and the dividing of time* (until all three harvests are completed; until the 144,000/Remnant is finally harvested into immortality). *(26) But the judgment shall sit, and they* (4th World Kingdom) *shall take away* (destroy) *his-*(the Devil's) *dominion, to consume and to destroy it unto the end. (27) And the kingdom and dominion, and the greatness of the kingdom under the whole heaven, shall be given to the people of the saints of the most High, whose kingdom is an everlasting kingdom, and all dominions shall serve and obey him. (28) Hitherto is the end of the matter..."*

And...

(Ref: Isa 3:25 – 4:4)–"(25) Your men-(of Israel) *shall fall by the sword, and your mighty in the war. (26) And her gates shall lament and mourn;*

and she being desolate (of Holy people) *shall sit upon the ground* (in the Sorrows-Period). (Ch. 4) *(1) And in that day* (end-time) *seven women* (the Seven Churches on earth?) *shall take hold of one man* (Jesus Christ?), *saying, We will eat our own bread, and wear our own apparel: only let us be called by your name, to take away our reproach. (2) In that day shall the* (devout) *branch of the lord be beautiful and glorious, and the fruit of the earth shall be excellent and comely for them that are escaped of Israel* (the 144,000/Remnant). *(3) And it shall come to pass, that he that is left in Zion, and he that remains in Jerusalem* (for the 1,000-Year-Reign), *shall be called holy* (the newly-Christianized 144,000/Remnant), *even every one that is written among the living in Jerusalem: (4) When the Lord shall have washed away the filth of the daughters of Zion* (through Tribulations-Period), *and shall have purged the blood of Jerusalem from the midst thereof by the Spirit of judgment, and by the Spirit of burning."*

And...

(Ref: Isa 24:14-23)—"(14) They shall lift up their voice, they shall sing for the majesty of the Lord, they shall cry aloud from the sea (during the Sorrows-Period). *(15) Wherefore glorify ye the Lord in the fires, even the name of the Lord God of Israel in the isles of the sea. (16) From the uttermost part of the earth have we heard songs* (the harpers harping and singing to the 144,000), *even glory to the righteous. But I said, My leanness, my leanness, woe unto me! the treacherous dealers have dealt treacherously; yea, the treacherous dealers have dealt very treacherously. (17) Fear, and the pit, and the snare, are upon you, o inhabitant of the Earth* (during the 3.5-year Tribulations-Period-[Seven Last Plagues of Wrath]). *(18) And it shall come to pass, that he who flees from the noise of the fear shall fall into the pit—*(i.e.; he who seeks to save his life, will lose it)*; and he that cometh up out of the midst of the pit shall be taken in the snare: for the windows from on high are open, and the foundations of the earth do shake. (19) The earth is utterly broken down,*

the earth is clean dissolved, the earth is moved exceedingly. (20) The earth shall reel to and fro like a drunkard, and shall be removed like a cottage; and the transgression thereof shall be heavy upon it; and it shall fall, and not rise again. (21) And it shall come to pass in that day, that the Lord shall punish the host of the high ones that are on high (the Authoritative Legions of Error/Evil that inhabits the Whore-souls), *and the kings of the earth upon the earth* (the Whore). *(22) And they shall be gathered together, as prisoners are gathered in the pit, and shall be shut up in the prison, and after many days shall they be visited. (23) Then the moon shall be confounded, and the sun ashamed, when the Lord of hosts shall reign in mount Zion, and in Jerusalem, and before his ancients gloriously."*

And...

(Ref: Zech 14:12-15)—"*(12) And this shall be the plague wherewith the Lord will smite all the people that have fought against Jerusalem*—(i.e.; offended the Kingdom of God); *their flesh shall consume away while they stand upon their feet, and their eyes shall consume away in their holes, and their tongue shall consume away in their mouth. (13) And it shall come to pass in that day, that a great tumult from the Lord shall be among them; and they (all the people that have fought against Jerusalem) shall lay hold every one on the hand of his neighbor, and his hand shall rise up against the hand of his neighbor. (14) And Judah also shall fight at Jerusalem; and the wealth of all the heathen round about shall be gathered together, gold, and silver, and apparel, in great abundance. (15) And so shall be the plague of the horse, of the mule, of the camel, and of the ass, and of all the Beasts that shall be in these tents, as this plague."*

CHAPTER 8 — THE HARVEST OF THE
144,000/REMNANT

Moving down the Revelation Grid—(See; Fig. 3 [pg. 39]), we find that at the end of Chapter 19 the prophecy discloses the manner in which the Lord will finally slay (and immortalize) the 144,000/Remnant (immediately after the Whore has been destroyed). **Rev 19:21** reads:

> "*(21)* **And the Remnant-**(144,000 Christianized Jews) **were slain with the sword of him that sat upon the horse** (Jesus)**, which sword proceeded out of his mouth** (the 'sword of the Lord'; his Word)**: and all the fowls were filled with their flesh** (also see; Math 24:27-28 & Luke 17:37)." — (See; Fig. 21 [pg. 238])

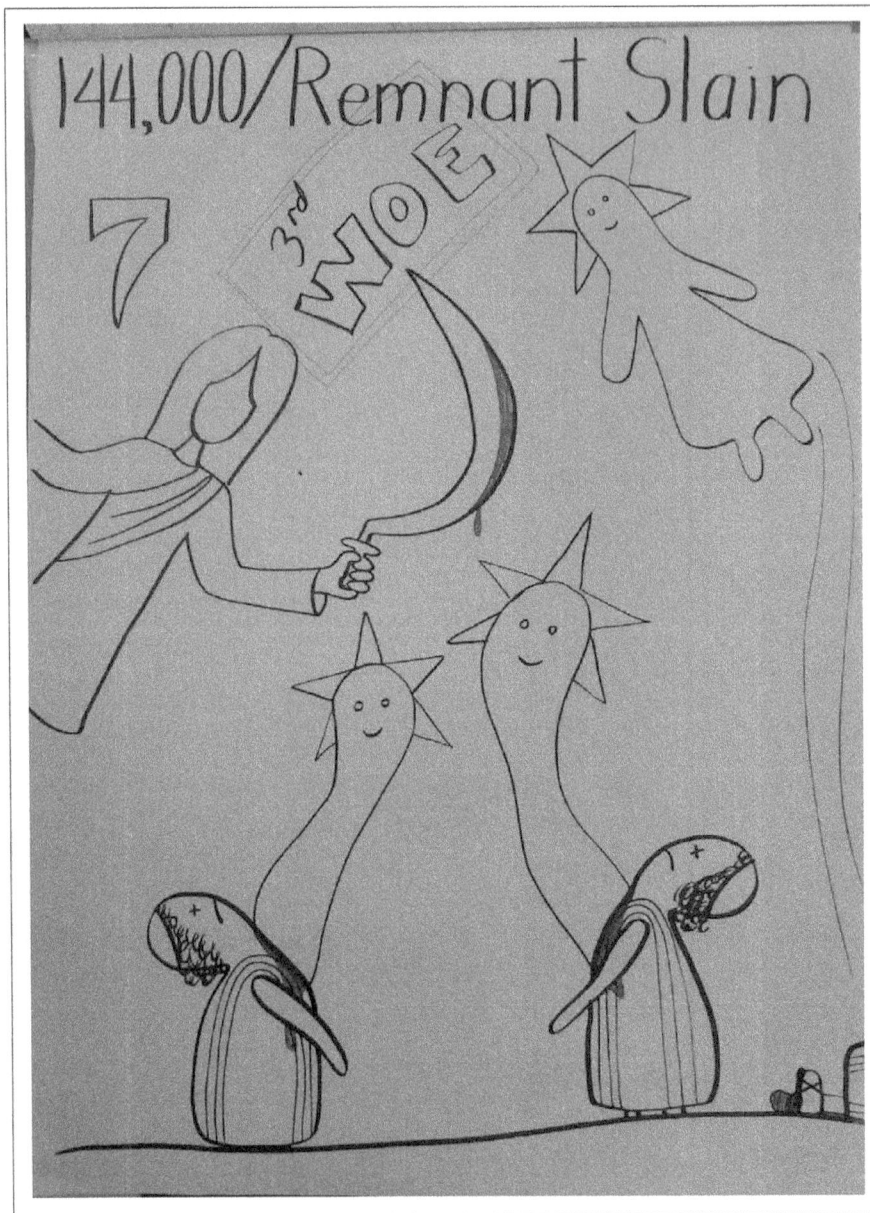

(Fig. 21 -- 144,000 Remnant Harvested)

These 144,000 souls will not 'sleep'-(be

dead/buried); they will simply be changed/immortalized

instantly (in the 'twinkling of an eye' [1 Cor

15:52]). And like all flesh of the end-times slaughters, the flesh of these 144,000 will be consumed by the fowl of Heaven. Consider the following verses which offer additional insight into this long-anticipated moment:

(Ref: 1 Cor 15:51-52)—"(51) Behold, I show you a mystery; We shall not all sleep-(lie dead/buried in graves), *but we shall all be changed-*(immortalized), *(52) In a moment, In the twinkling of an eye, at the last trump-*(Seventh Trump): *for the trumpet shall sound, and the dead-*(slain/immortalized) *shall be raised incorruptible, and we shall be changed."*

And...

(Ref: Isa 11:11)—"And it shall come to pass in that day, that the Lord shall set His hand (prepare the stage) *again the second time-(at the Seventh Trump) to recover the Remnant of his people* (the 144,000), *which shall be left* (left behind from the Sixth Trump-harvest [of Christian-Witnesses])..."*

And...

(Ref: Jer 16:14-16)—"(14) Therefore, behold, the days come, says the Lord, that it shall no more be said, The Lord lives, that brought up the children of Israel out of the land of Egypt; (15) But, (rather) The Lord lives, that brought up the children of Israel from the land of the north, and from all the lands whither he had driven them: and I will bring them again into their land that I gave unto their fathers. (16) Behold, I will send for many fishers-(immortalized Christian teachers), *says the Lord, and they shall fish them-*(the 144,000)*; and after will I send for many hunters-*(angels of God)*, and they shall hunt them from every mountain, and from every hill, and out of the holes of the rocks."*
And...

(Ref: Isa 1:27)—"Zion-(the end-time devout, of Israel) *shall be redeemed with judgment* (tried, through Tribulations-Period)*, and her converts-*(those Christianized) *with righteousness* (through grace)."*
And...

(Ref: Jer 46:27-28)—"(27) But fear not thou, O my servant Jacob, and be not dismayed, O Israel: for, behold, I will save you from afar off, and your seed from the land of their captivity; and Jacob shall return, and be in rest and at ease, and none shall make him afraid. (28) Fear you not, O Jacob my servant, says the Lord: for I am with you; for I will make a full end of all the nations whither I have driven you: but I will not make a full end of you, but correct you in measure; yet will I not leave you wholly unpunished—(i.e.; the 144,000/Remnant will have to endure temptation [and exhibit faith and obedience] through the Tribulations-Period, to be redeemed)."

And...

(Ref: Isa 14:1-2)—"(1) For the Lord will have mercy on Jacob, and will yet choose Israel, and set them in their own land (for the 1,000-Year-Reign): *and the strangers* (the Lukewarm who remain on earth with them, after Armageddon) *shall be joined with them, and they shall cleave to the house of Jacob. (2) And the people-*(the

144,000/Remnant) *shall take them, and bring them to their place: and the house of Israel shall possess them-*(the Lukewarm) *in the land of the Lord for servants and handmaids: and they shall take them captives, whose captives they were; and they shall rule over their oppressors* (Lukewarm authority)*."*

And...

(Ref: Dan 12:6-12)—"(6) And one said to the man clothed in linen, which was upon the waters of the river, how long shall it be to the end of these wonders? (7) And I heard the man clothed in linen, which was upon the waters of the river, when he held up his right hand and his left hand unto heaven, and swore by him that lives for ever that it shall be for a time, times, and an half—(i.e.; it shall be until all three harvests have been completed)*; and when he shall have accomplished to scatter the power of the holy people* (into the 144,000/Remnant)*, all these things shall be finished. (8) And I heard, but I understood not: then said I, O my Lord, what shall be the end of these things? (9) And he*

said, Go your way, Daniel: for the Words are
closed up and sealed till the time of the end.
(10) Many shall be purified, and made white, and
tried (through the seven-year
Sorrows/Tribulations-Period)*; but the wicked*
shall do wickedly: and none of the wicked shall
understand; but the wise shall understand. (11)
And from the time that the daily sacrifice shall
be taken away—(i.e.; from the time the Christian-
Witnesses-[Body of Christ] are killed)*, and the*
abomination that maketh desolate set up—(i.e.;
the armies of Error/Evil surrounding Jerusalem-
[Kingdom of God], *there shall be a thousand two*
hundred and ninety days (3.5 years). *(12) Blessed*
is he that waits, and comes to the thousand three
hundred and five and thirty days (3.7-year
mark)."

In Dan 12, above, verses 11-12 tell us that from
the harvest of the Christian-Witnesses, to the harvest
of the 144,000/Remnant, there will be 3.5 years of
time (this is the Tribulations-Period-[Seven Plagues
of Wrath]). We already learned (in Rev 11:3) that the
Christian-Witnesses will be killed at the end of the

3.5-year Sorrows-Period. These verses verify the end time scenario of a seven-year period of Sorrows/Tribulations, in the middle of which; the Two Witnesses-(Christian-Witnesses) are harvested from the Earth.

In review: The Christian population/Church is harvested from the earth (to the Sea of Glass) and given immortalized bodies. From there, they will proceed to minister to the 144,000 on Mt. Zion throughout the Seven Last Plagues of Wrath-(Tribulations-Period). Three and one half years (3.5 years) later, the Whore population of the world will be destroyed (souls that had been indwelled by Beast-[Legions of Error/Evil] and Antichrist-[Voice of Error/Evil]). Immediately after the Whore is destroyed, the 144,000/Remnant will be slain (receiving their immortalized bodies [to live on Mt. Zion/Earth during the 1,000-Year-Reign]). The only mortal souls that will remain (alive) on Earth (with the immortalized 144,000) during the upcoming 1,000-Year-Reign are the Lukewarms-(self-worshippers).

Remember; the Lukewarms will become so fed up with the stifling demands of Christian standards that they willingly look the other way when the Whore rises up to destroy the Christian-Witnesses. But soon afterward, they find themselves stuck with the equally demanding Whore. And, when they finally have all they can tolerate of oppressive Whore-mankind, they will rise up and destroy the Whore (at God's prompting). The next thing they know, the stifling (Christianized) 144,000/Remnant are immortalized and set in the place of authority over the Earth (and, them). Then, they are commanded to serve the will of God (and the immortalized Kingdom) on Mt. Zion for the next 1,000 years; forced to neglect the desires of their own wills. These self-worshipping Lukewarms will be ripe for the picking when the Devil is released from the Bottomless Pit at the end of the 1,000-Year-Reign.

Moving down the Revelation Grid—(See; Fig. 3 [pg. 39]), we see that Chapter 16 discusses a division of the great city into three parts. I am not yet convinced of exactly who the 'great city' refers to, in this verse. It could be referring to the three components of Babylon (having now been dismantled): the Antichrist-Voice, the Beast/Legion-of-Error, and the Whore they indwelled. Alternatively, it could possibly be referring to the three harvests of the Kingdom of God (which, have by now been completed). Last but not least; 'great city' could be referring to the three man-groups of the world, in general (the Good, the Evil and the Unaffiliated/Lukewarms; which have now been compartmentalized into three manageable groups). **Rev 16:19-21** goes on, to say:

> "*(19)* ***And the great city*** (Babylon; reign of Error/Evil?) ***was divided into three parts, and the cities*** (bodies?) ***of the nations fell: and great Babylon-***(the Whore-presence of the 4th Kingdom) ***came in remembrance before God, to give unto her the cup of wine of the fierceness of His wrath*** (her complete destruction). *(20)* ***And*** (during that time) ***every island fled away, and the mountains were not found.*** *(21)* ***And*** (during that time) ***there fell upon men a great hail out of heaven, every stone about the weight of a talent: and*** (during that time) ***men*** (Whore-mankind) ***blasphemed God because of the plague of the hail; for the plague thereof was exceeding great.***"

Moving down and across the Revelation Grid—(See; Fig. 3 [pg. 39]), we see that after painting such an horrific and detailed portrait of how the Whore will be destroyed in the end time, the prophecy now takes a reflective turn to lay out the entire mystery of the Whore; from beginning to end. **Rev 17:1-6** reads:

"*(1)* ***And there came one of the seven angels which had the seven vials, and talked with me, saying unto me, Come hither; I will shew unto you the judgment of the great Whore***-(bride of Legion; Evil world power) ***that sits upon many waters:*** *(2)* ***With whom the kings of the earth have committed fornication, and the inhabitants of the earth have been made drunk with the wine of her fornication.*** *(3)* ***So He carried me away in the spirit into the wilderness***-(the place of ungodly mankind)*:* ***and I saw a Woman*** (collective-Whore) ***sit upon a scarlet colored Beast***—(i.e.; she was 'powered' by the Beast/Legions of Error/Evil), ***full of names of blasphemy, having seven heads***-(continents) ***and ten horns*** (ten Lukewarm Kings)—(i.e.; Whore-mankind sits upon the Earth, powered by the Beast [which is stained by the blood of the Saints] and is supplemented by the power of ten Lukewarm Kings). *(4) And the Woman was arrayed in purple and scarlet color, and decked with gold and precious stones and pearls, having a golden cup in her hand full of abominations and filthiness of her fornication. (5) And upon her forehead was a name written, mystery, Babylon the great*-(the Antichrist-empowered/Authoritative Whore-soul of mankind; the 4th Kingdom of the world), *the mother of harlots and abominations of the Earth. (6) And I saw the Woman* (Collective-Whore; bride of Legion) *drunken with the blood of the saints, and with the blood of the martyrs of Jesus: and when I saw her, I wondered with great admiration* (awe)." — (See; Fig. 22 [pg. 249])

(**Rev 17:7-8** goes on, to say):

"*(7) And the angel said unto me, Wherefore didst you marvel* (about the vision)*? I will tell you the mystery of the Woman*-(collective-Whore), *and of the Beast*-(Legions of Error/Evil) *that carries her, which hath the seven heads*-(continents) *and ten horns* (ten Lukewarm Kings). *(8) The Beast*-(Legions of Error/Evil) *that you saw was, and is*

(Fig. 22 -- Mystery of the Whore, Revealed)

not; and shall ascend out of the Bottomless Pit (over and over)**, and go into perdition**-(the world)**: and they that dwell on the earth shall**

wonder, whose names were not written in the book of life from the foundation of the world—(i.e.; the Whore & Lukewarm will wonder), *when they behold the Beast that was, and is not, and yet is*—(i.e.; the Legion [of Error/Evil] that keeps returning, from the Abyss)." — (See; Fig. 22 [pg. 249])

In Review: When the Christian-Witnesses are destroyed (at end of Sorrows-Period), the devout of Judaism (144,000) are awakened to Jesus (transitioning out of the mindset/church of Smyrna [Judaism]; converting into the mindset/Church of Philadelphia [Christianity]). Here, the 'two flocks' of God become one flock; suggesting that the Church of Smyrna (Judaism; the 'First-Amendment-only' religion) will no longer stand, beyond this point. When the Whore is destroyed at the end of the Tribulations-Period, four more churches fall (the churches of Ephesus, Pergamos, Thyatira and Sardis). This will leave only two churches entering into the 1,000-Year-Reign on Earth; Philadelphia-(144,000 Christianized Jews) and Laodicea-(the Lukewarms). At the end of the 1,000-Year-Reign, the Lukewarm church will also fall (when they finally agree to take a stand with the Devil against the Kingdom of God). **Rev 17:9-14** goes on, to say:

"*(9) And here is the mind which hath wisdom. The seven heads are seven mountains* (seven continents, rising out of the sea)*, on which the Woman*-(Collective-Whore [world power]) *sits. (10) And there are seven kings*-(seven mindsets of mankind [churches at issue, before the throne of God])*: five are fallen*—(i.e.; lost their candlesticks, by this point in the Seventh Seal events)*, and one is* (in right standing with God [the mindset of Philadelphia; Christianized mankind])*, and the other* (mindset of Laodicea; the Lukewarms) *is not yet come* (into allegiance to God or Devil)*; and when he cometh, he must continue a short space* (to rise up against the 144,000 with the Devil)*. (11) And the Beast*-(Legions of Error/Evil) *that was, and is not, even he is the eighth* (king/mindset)*, and is of the seven* (kings/mindsets)*, and goes into perdition*-(the world)*. (12) And the ten horns which you saw are ten* (Lukewarm) *kings, which* *have received no kingdom yet* (no reign, by this point in the Seventh Seal events)*; but* (will) *receive power as kings one hour with the Beast* (which was, and is not...and yet, is). *(13) These* (Lukewarm kings) *have one mind* (rebellion against the Kingdom of God)*, and shall give their power and strength unto the Beast* (when the Beastly Devil is released from the Pit at the end of the 1,000-Year-Reign). *(14) These* (the ten Lukewarm kings and the Devil's Beastly spirit of Error) *shall make war with the lamb* (surrounding Jesus and the 144,000/Kingdom on Mt. Zion [Earth])*, and the Lamb shall overcome them: for he is lord of lords, and King of kings: and they that are with him* (on Mt. Zion) *are called, and chosen, and faithful*—(i.e.; God will devour the Beastly Devil and the Lukewarm/Magog-converts] with fire from Heaven; setting the Earth ablaze)." — (See; Fig. 22 [pg. 249])

The Legions of Error/Evil are dark angels. The Devil, himself, is a dark angel. Therefore, it is not a stretch for me to interpret the 'Beast' mentioned in the above passages to be referring to the Devil, himself, this time (since we know that by now the originally-mentioned Beast/Legion has long since been imprisoned in the Lake of Fire).

This would also be a good time for us to take a long, deep look into the Lukewarm-mindset, in general. Throughout history, the (self-worshipping) Lukewarm-souls have had godly people chewing on one ear (pressuring them to support what is good/right [even when those things aren't particularly convenient for the Lukewarms]), and they've also had Evil/Error-(the oppressive Whore) chewing on their other ear (pressuring them to help derail any foothold that good/right principles manage to achieve in the world [even when that battle isn't particularly convenient for the Lukewarms]). But the Lukewarm-mindset has always been aggravated by both of these 'would-be' bosses/authorities; they just want to live and let live (independent of good or evil stigmatisms). They don't want to honor other people's moral standards or agendas — just mankind's right to self-satisfy, in general; everyone minding their own business.

In review: At the end of the 3.5-year Sorrows-Period; the Lukewarm kings (convinced that the stifling demands of Christianity are responsible for at least half of world conflict) passively allow the Whore-Movement to eradicate all the Christian-Witnesses from the Earth — and they celebrate their destruction. But immediately afterward, they find themselves being completely dominated and oppressed by unrestrained Error/Evil (through the Whore). After enduring the violence and chaos of the conscienceless Whore for the next 3.5 years (throughout the Tribulations-Period-[Seven Last Plagues of Wrath]) the Lukewarms rise up (behind the scenes) and lend themselves to the destruction of the Whore (during the battle of Armageddon; the second Whore-Movement). This is a covert action which God, Himself, actually compels and facilitates (through the Lukewarms), to accomplish His own end-goal; the destruction of the Whore. When God then goes on to immortalize the 144,000/Remnant (immediately after Armageddon), the Lukewarms-(self-worshippers) find themselves (once again) stuck sharing the Earth with the Kingdom of God. With no desire or intention to ever truly conform to the will of God (to sincerely serve Him), the Lukewarms serve the Kingdom begrudgingly for the next

1,000 years (throughout the 1,000-Year-Reign of Jesus, on Earth).

When the Devil is released from the Bottomless Pit (at the end of the 1,000-Year-Reign), and his Beastly spirit-[Voice of Error/Evil] rises up to convince the Lukewarm population of Earth that (together) they can take back the world — the Lukewarms will welcome his partnership; agreeing to rise up with him against the Kingdom of God. Thus, Magog-(the Lukewarm mindset) will convert to sold-out Evil/Error-(Gog) and move to initiate the third (final) Whore-Movement on Earth; powered and guided by Satan's Beastly spirit, they will surround the immortalized Kingdom/144,000 on Mt. Zion; prepared to attack. But, they will be instantly devoured by fire from God (having finally made their free-will choice between God and Satan, and acted on it).

Getting back to our Revelation text; Chapter 17 continues unveiling the 'mystery' of the Whore (from the point where the Lukewarms rise up to destroy the Whore). **Rev 17:15-18** goes on, to say:

"*(15)* ***And he***-(the same angel that has been speaking to John) ***says unto me*** (regarding the vision of the Whore riding the seven-headed Beast), *the waters which you saw, where the Whore sits, are peoples, and multitudes, and nations, and tongues*—(i.e.; the Beast rises up through the people; to live sumptuously through the Whore). *(16) And the ten horns* (the ten Lukewarm kings) *which you saw upon the Beast*-(Legions of Error/Evil), *these shall* (come to) *hate the Whore, and shall make her desolate and naked* (at Armageddon), *and* (these ten Lukewarm kings) *shall eat her flesh, and burn her with fire. (17) For God hath put it in their hearts to fulfill His will* (to destroy the committed bride of Legion), *and to agree, and give their kingdom*-(their allegiance) *unto the Beast* (partner with Evil), *until the Words of God shall be fulfilled. (18) And the Woman which you saw is that great city*-(Babylon, the empowered/Authoritative Whore-soul of mankind; the 4th Kingdom of the world), *which reigns over* (oppresses) *the kings of the earth."* — (See; Fig. 22 [pg. 249])

Moving down the Revelation Grid; Chapter 20 resumes our actual sequence of end-time events;

picking back up where the Dragon-[the Devil] is bound up and imprisoned after the 144,000 are immortalized (for the 1,000-Year-Reign). **Rev 20:1-3** reads:

"*(1) and I saw an angel come down from heaven, having the key of the Bottomless Pit and a great chain in his hand. (2) And he laid hold on the Dragon, that old Serpent*-(Father of Error/Evil), *which is the Devil, and Satan, and bound him a thousand years*—(i.e.; for the 1,000-Year-Reign), *(3) And cast him into the Bottomless Pit, and shut him up, and set a seal upon him, that he* (Error/Evil) *should deceive the nations no more*—(i.e.; the Devil's spirit [of Error/Evil] will not be able to influence the Lukewarm or the 144,000 in any way, for the next 1,000 years), *till the thousand years should be fulfilled: and after that he* (Error/Evil) *must be loosed a little season.*" — (See; Fig. 23 [pg. 258])

Finally; the 1,000-Year-Reign begins. **Rev 20:4-6** reads:

"*(4) And I saw thrones* (in Heaven)*, and they sat upon them* (the Christian-Witnesses and Saints, In Heaven)*, and judgment was given unto them*

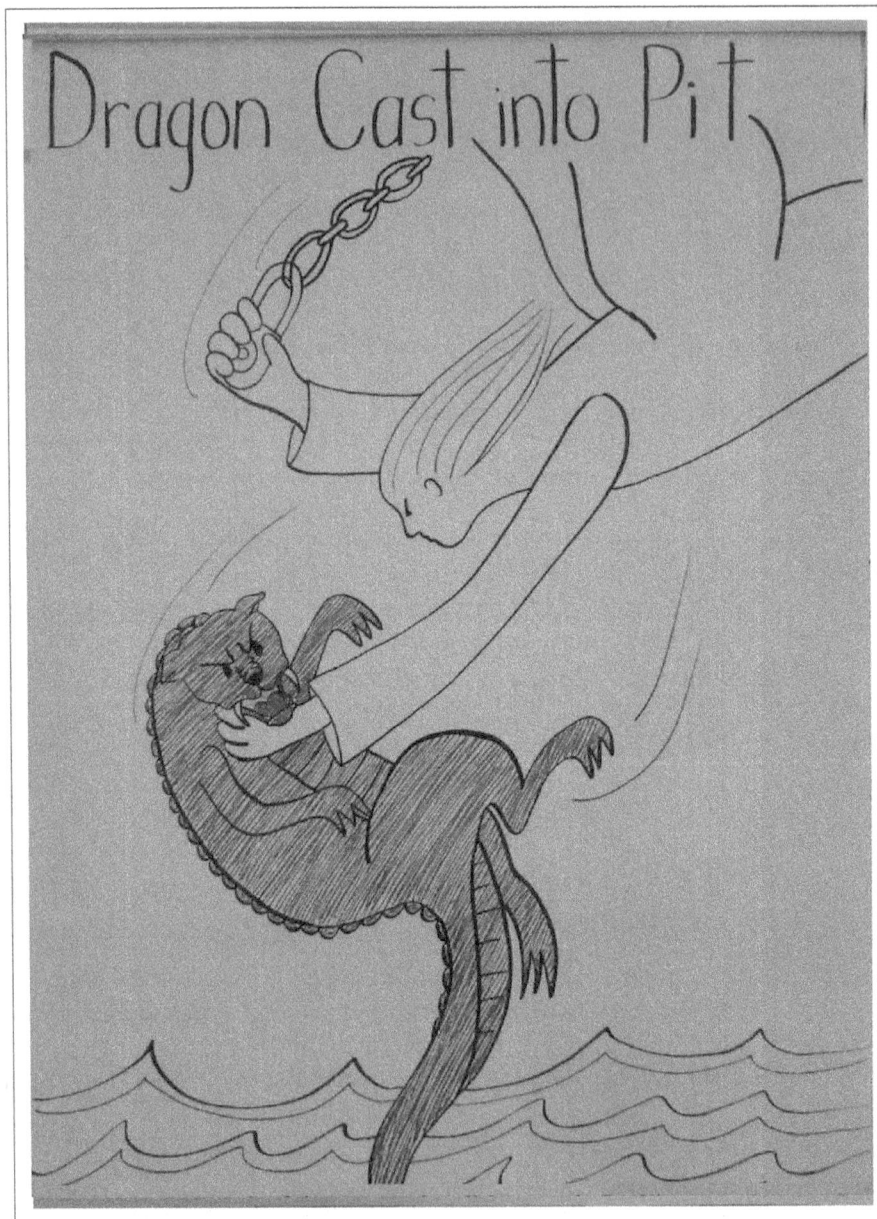

(Fig. 23; Dragon Cast into Bottomless Pit)

(authority to judge): **and I saw the souls of them**
(the 144,000/Remnant) **that were beheaded for the**
Witness of Jesus, and for the Word of God, and

which had not worshipped-(feared and obeyed) *the Beast*-(Legions of Error/Evil)*, neither his image*-(the Whores of Error/Evil)*, neither had received his mark upon their foreheads, or in their hands*—(i.e.; neither had been assessed as an offense against the Word of God or His people; assessed as part of the Beast [by their mindset or behavior])*; and they* (the immortalized 144,000/Remnant) *lived and reigned with Christ a thousand years* (on Mt. Zion). *(5) But the rest of the dead*—(i.e.; the sleeping souls of the dead/buried 'damned') *lived not again until the thousand years were finished* (when they will be resurrected into the White-Throne Judgement and eternal damnation). *This is the first resurrection* (verse 4, above; the resurrection of the Just [eternal life]). *(6) Blessed and holy is he that hath part in the first resurrection: on such the second death* (verse 5, above; the resurrection of the Damned [eternal death]) *hath no power, but they shall be priests of God and of Christ, and shall reign with him a thousand years.*" — (See; Fig. 24 [pg. 260])

(Fig. 24 -- 1,000-Year Reign)

As we see in verse 5, above, all the buried souls of the damned will remain in the grave-(Hell) throughout the 1,000-Year-Reign. Afterward, they will be resurrected from the grave to face Christ at the White Throne Judgement (at which point, every damned soul will also be cast into the Lake of Fire). The resurrected Christian-Witnesses and Saints (the 'Just') will have already been judged, long ago (at the time of their own resurrection). Consider the following verses which discuss the 1,000-Year-Reign:

> *(Ref: Zech 14:16-19)—"(16) And it shall come to pass, that every one that is left of all the nations which came against Jerusalem* (rebelled against the Kingdom) *shall even go up from year to year* (the Lukewarms) *to worship the King, the Lord of hosts, and to keep the feast of tabernacles* (along with the 144,000). *(17) And it shall be, that whoso will not come up of all the* (Lukewarm) *families of the earth unto Jerusalem to worship the King, the Lord of hosts, even upon them shall be no rain. (18) And if the family of Egypt go not up, and come not, that have no rain; there shall be the plague, wherewith the Lord will smite the heathen that come not up to keep the feast of tabernacles. (19) This shall be the punishment of Egypt, and the punishment of all*

nations that come not up to keep the feast of
tabernacles."

And...

(Ref: Isa 14:1-2)—"(1) For the Lord will have
mercy on Jacob, and will yet choose Israel
(144,000), *and set them in their own land* (for
the 1,000-Year-Reign): *and the strangers* (the
Lukewarm who remain on earth with them, after
Armageddon) *shall be joined with them, and they*
shall cleave to the house of Jacob (having no
choice). *(2) And the people-*(the 144,000/Remnant)
shall take them, and bring them to their place:
and the house of Israel shall possess them-(the
Lukewarm) *in the land of the Lord for servants*
and handmaids: and they shall take them captives,
whose captives they were; and they shall rule
over their oppressors."

And...

(Ref: Mic 4:1-4)—"(1) But in the last days it
shall come to pass, that the mountain of the
house of the Lord shall be established in the top
of the mountains, and it-(Mt. Zion) *shall be*
exalted above the hills; and people shall flow

unto it. (2) And many nations (the Lukewarms) *shall come, and say* (only because they have no choice)*, Come, and let us go up to the mountain of the Lord, and to the house of the God of Jacob; and he will teach us of his ways, and we will walk in his paths: for the law shall go forth of Zion, and the Word of the Lord from Jerusalem. (3) And He shall judge among many people, and rebuke strong* (Lukewarm) *nations afar off; and they shall beat their swords into plowshares, and their spears into pruninghooks: nation shall not lift up a sword against nation, neither shall they learn war any more. (4) But they shall sit every man under his vine and under his fig tree; and none shall make them afraid: for the mouth of the Lord of hosts hath spoken it*—(Also, see; Ezek Ch. 40 — Ch. 48)."
And...

(Ref: Ezek 34:25-26)—"*(25) And I will make with them* (the 144,000) *a covenant of peace, and will cause the Evil Beasts to cease out of the land: and they shall dwell safely in the wilderness, and sleep in the woods. (26) And I will make them and the places round about my hill-(Zion) a blessing; and I will cause the shower to come down in His season; there shall be showers of blessing."*

And...

(Ref: Jer 50:19-20)—"(19) And I will bring Israel again to his habitation, and He shall feed on Carmel and Bashan, and his soul shall be satisfied upon mount Ephraim and Gilead. (20) In those days, and in that time, says the Lord, the iniquity of Israel shall be sought for, and there shall be none; and the sins of Judah, and they shall not be found: for I will pardon them whom I reserve."

And...

(Ref: Jer 31:8-14)—"(8) Behold, I will bring them from the north country, and gather them from the coasts of the earth, and with them the blind and the lame, the Woman with child and her that travails with child together: a great company shall return thither (prior to the 1,000-Year-Reign)...they shall come and sing in the height of Zion, and shall flow together to the Goodness

of the Lord, for wheat, and for wine, and for oil, and for the young of the flock and of the herd: and their soul shall be as a watered garden; and they shall not sorrow any more at all (during the 1,000-Year-Reign). (13) Then shall the virgin rejoice in the dance, both young men and old together: for I will turn their mourning into joy, and will comfort them, and make them rejoice from their sorrow. (14) And I will satiate the soul of the priests with fatness, and my people shall be satisfied with my Goodness, says the Lord."

And...

(Ref: Jer 32:37-42)—"(37) Behold, I will gather them-(the 144,000) *out of all countries, whither I have driven them in mine anger, and in my fury, and in great wrath; and I will bring them again unto this place, and I will cause them to dwell safely: (38) And they shall be my people, and I will be their God: (39) And I will give them one heart* (the heart-amendment; New Testament Word)*, and one way, that they may fear me for ever, for the good of them, and of their children after*

them: (40) And I will make an everlasting covenant with them, that I will not turn away from them, to do them good; but I will put my fear in their hearts, that they shall not depart from me. (41) Yea, I will rejoice over them to do them good, and I will plant them in this land assuredly with my whole heart and with my whole soul. (42) For thus says the Lord; Like as I have brought all this great Evil upon this people, so will I bring upon them all the good that I have promised them."

CHAPTER 9 — END OF THE 1,000-YEAR-REIGN

For the entire duration of the 1,000-Year-Reign, the disgruntled Lukewarm-(self-worshipping) population of the Earth will be the captive servants of the immortalized Kingdom of God (on Mt. Zion), and the Devil-(Father of Error/Evil) will be detained under lock and key in the Bottomless Pit (with his Antichrist Voice of Error/Evil and his Legions of Error/Evil smoldering in the Lake of Fire). Error/Evil will be unable to influence the Lukewarm-souls in any way, for 1,000 years. When the Devil-(Error/Evil) is released from the Pit (at the end of the 1,000-Year-Reign); true to his nature, he will go immediately out into the world (his Spirit of Error/Evil) to seduce the disgruntled Lukewarm servants into revolt against the immortalized Kingdom of God (the 144,000 on Mt. Zion). **Rev 20:7-8** tells us what happens when he is released:

> "*(7)* ***And when the thousand years are expired, Satan shall be loosed out of his prison, (8) And shall go out to deceive the*** (Lukewarm) ***nations which are in the four quarters of the earth,*** (seducing) ***Gog-***(those souls formerly 'Lukewarm' who will have changed their mindset [during the 1,000-Year-Reign] to fully embrace Error/Evil) ***and Magog-***(the remaining Lukewarms who [thus far] still remain neutral)***, to gather them together to battle: the number of whom is as the sand of the sea.***" — (See; Fig. 25 [pg. 269])

When the Devil re-enters the Earth to seduce the Lukewarms (and her Evil-converts) they will not hesitate to marry themselves to him (for the chance to get out from under the stifling thumb of the Kingdom of God). And once they finally align themselves with the Devil (in movement against God's Kingdom) God will immediately destroy them; setting the whole world on fire. **Rev 20:9-10** reads:

(Fig. 25 -- 3rd 'Whore-Movement'; Dragon's Last Stand)

"*(9)* **And they**-(the Devil, the Lukewarms and the Evil-converts) **went up on the breadth of the Earth, and compassed the saints about, and the**

beloved city (i.e.; they staged themselves for the third Whore-Movement; surrounding the 144,000/Remnant of Israel)***: and*** (immediately) ***fire came down from God out of Heaven, and devoured them*** (engulfing the whole Earth in flames)—(See; Fig. 10[d] [pg. 271]). *(10)* ***And the Devil*** -(Father of Error/Evil) ***that deceived them was cast into the Lake of Fire and brimstone, where the Beast*** -(Legions of Error/Evil) ***and the false prophet*** -(Antichrist Voice of Error/Evil) ***are, and shall be tormented day and night for ever and ever*** (burning, within the flaming 'Morning Star')." — (See; Fig. 25 [pg. 269])

As we see in the verses above, the Devil's last battle never does take place. Consider the following (Old Testament) prophecies, which discuss the Devil's (unavoidable) final disposition:

(Ref: Isa 14:12)—"How are you fallen from Heaven, o Lucifer, Son of the Morning (star)! how are you cut down to the ground, which didst weaken the nations!"

And...

On The Earth	In The Grave	On The Sea of Glass	In The Lake of Fire
'Devout' Jews (144,000) 'Lukewarm Mankind'	Buried Sinners /Whore	Early Saints Christian Witnesses Buried Saints	Beast & False Prophet (Antichrist) Beastly Devil

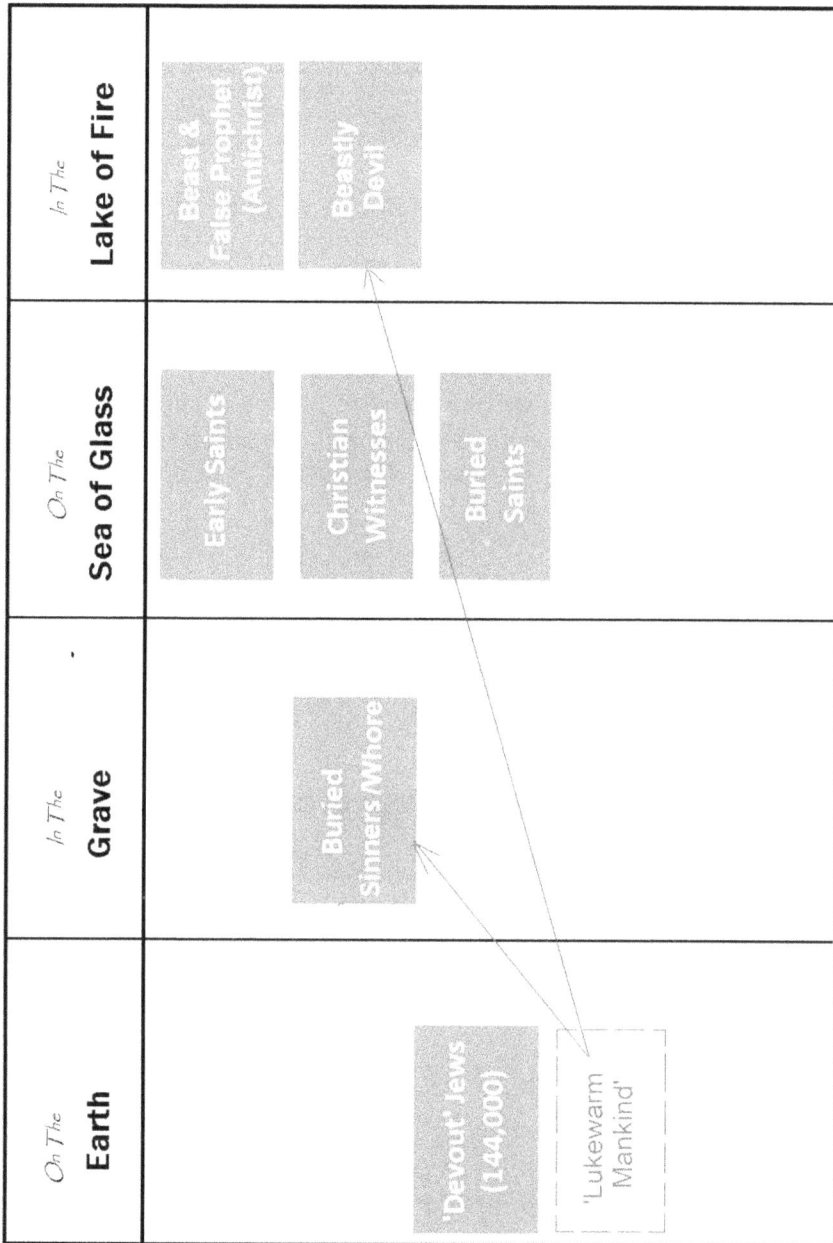

(Fig. 10d — Lukewarm-Mankind is Killed)

(Ref: Isa 27:1)—"In that day the Lord with his sore and great and strong sword shall punish Leviathan the piercing Serpent, even leviathan *that crooked Serpent; and he shall slay the Dragon that is in the sea."*

From today's perspective; God will wait until every single human being has made their free-will choice between Him and the Devil, then He will finally cast the Devil (his lying Spirit of Error/Evil) into the Lake of Fire. Afterward, God will resurrect every damned soul from their graves, and bring them forth to judge them at the great White-Throne Judgment (in Heaven). As we saw in earlier passages, the Just were already judged (at the end of the Sorrows-Period). **Rev 20:11-15** goes on, to say:

*"(11) **And I saw a great White Throne, and him that sat on it, from whose face the** (former) **earth and the** (former) **heaven fled away**—(i.e.; Earth and Heaven, as we know them, are now gone); **and there was found no place for them. (12) And I saw the dead, small and great, stand before God** (resurrected); **and the books were opened: and another book was opened, which is the Book of Life** (to verify their names are not in there): **and the dead** (the damned) **were judged out of those things which were written in the books,***

*according to their works. (13) **And the sea gave up the dead which were in it; and death and Hell-**(the grave) **delivered up the dead which were in them: and they were judged every man according to their works. (14) And Death and Hell were cast into the Lake of Fire. This is the second death. (15) And whosoever was not found written in the Book of Life was cast into the Lake of Fire."* — (See; Fig. 25 [pg. 269])

In the Second Death (the death of the damned), those unfortunate souls don't actually expire or disappear (or, even sleep). Instead; the death of the damned is actually an eternal existence burning in the Lake of Fire (the prison God designed for Satan and his dark angels)—(See; Fig. 10[e] [pg. 274]).

Many people believe that when a person dies, their soul goes either to Heaven or to (fiery) Hell, immediately. In my study of the scriptures, I have not found this to be the case. Again; I understand the scriptures to provide this pattern of events: When a person's flesh-(the physical-component of soul) dies, their will-(the spiritual-component of soul) goes to sleep. When this happens, their spiritual-husband-(the

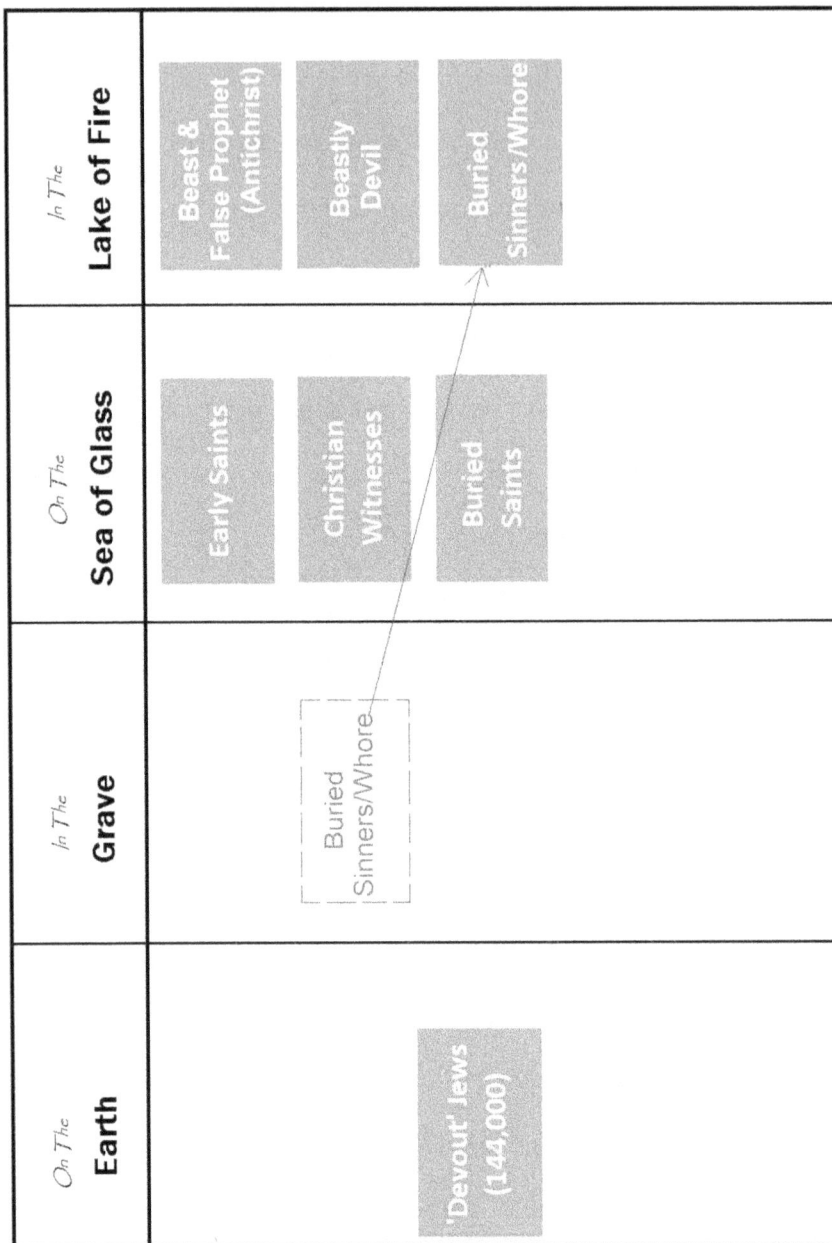

(Fig. 10e – Resurrected Sinners are Cast into Lake of Fire)

partner they chose in life; Good or Evil) separates

himself from the sleeping will-(soul) and returns to

his origin—(i.e.; to Heaven or to the Abyss). Asleep,

each (spiritual)-soul/will remains, until God

resurrects them (wakes them up) to judge them.
Consider the following verse which explains very
clearly the state of a deceased soul:

(Ref: Job 14:12-15)—"*(12) So man lies down* (dies,
and is buried), *and rises not: till the Heavens
be no more*—(i.e.; asleep, till God resurrects
them in the end-time), *they shall not awake, nor
be raised out of their sleep. (13) O that you
would hide me in the grave* (let me go to sleep,
now), *that you would keep me secret, until your
wrath be past, that you would appoint me a set
time, and remember me* (resurrect me)*! (14) If a
man die, shall he live again? all the days of my
appointed time will I wait, till my change-*
(immortalization) *come. (15) you shall call, and
I will answer you* (from the grave)*: you will have
a desire to(ward) the work of thine hands*—(i.e.;
toward the souls you have created)."

In the above verse, Job is begging God to end his
life (and his suffering) — knowing that when he
awakens again, it will be for eternity (in a much
better place). Job understood that when men die, they
remain asleep-(in their grave) until God resurrects

them (according to His harvest schedule-[the 'time', 'times' and 'the dividing of time']).

Many people are confused about this issue because they understand Jesus to have told the thief (on the cross) that he-(the thief's soul) would be in Paradise with Jesus the very day they both died (Luke 23:43). There are four problems with using that passage as a point of reference: (1) The Bible is very clear that Jesus spent three days and nights in the grave, before he was even resurrected (Matt 12:40). In other words; not even Jesus, himself, would be in Heaven/Paradise the same day that he died — let alone, would the thief be in Paradise with him; (2) Four days after Jesus died, the resurrected Jesus, himself, told the women visiting his tomb; "Do not touch me yet, for I have not yet ascended to my Father (in Paradise) (John 20:17)." (In other words: four days after Jesus and the thief died, Jesus states that he 'still' has not risen to Paradise; (3) In all; the resurrected Jesus remained on the Earth (visiting His apostles) for a total of forty days after his resurrection, before finally being raised into Heaven/Paradise (from Bethany/Mount-of-Olives) [Luke 24:46-51]), and; (4)

the statement Jesus made to the thief on the cross was originally quoted to us from Greek texts (a written language that contains no punctuation marks). Bearing this tiny (albeit, important) piece of knowledge in mind, it is reasonable to conclude that this issue doesn't necessarily have to represent either an error in the Word of God, or, an undiscoverable mystery of Truth. It is not beyond the realm of possibility that the early translators simply miss-punctuated Jesus' statement (and clearly; did).

In response to the thief's request (that Jesus promise to receive him into Heaven when He takes the throne) I believe Jesus actually answered; *"I tell you, today; 'you shall be with me in Paradise.'"* This statement rings true throughout the scriptures, because it implies; "In the light of this atoning day, I say to you; 'You will be with me in Paradise.'"

Some theologians use a different Bible reference to argue their contention that dead/buried souls do not necessarily sleep undisturbed in a grave until resurrected in the end-time. These, quote the scripture where King Saul uses a Medium-(a paranormal vessel/person) to raise the dead/buried-(sleeping) prophet, Samuel, to talk to King Saul (1 Samuel 28:12-15).

There are two problems with using this passage as a point of reference: (1) The above-mentioned verses clearly state that 'gods' (plural & uncapitalized) brought Samuel up out of his sleep; not 'God' (who, alone, has the power of resurrection). And for the 'gods' (of the earth)—(i.e.; the dark angels) to bring forth this type of familiar-spirit (just to abase Saul) makes more sense to me than the likelihood that dark angels have the power to resurrect and harass God's sleeping saints, and; (2) These passages clearly state that it was the woman/Medium (alone) who 'saw' the spirit which was raised. In other words; only the ungodly-woman saw the spirit (and then described it to Saul) — then, Saul simply presumed the spirit to be Samuel (based on the Woman's description of what she saw). For all the reasons stated above, I conclude that there is no biblical support [at all] for the belief that Jesus (and/or the thief) appeared in Paradise the very day they died.

Returning to the Revelation text; by this point in the sequence of end-time events, all of Godly-mankind has been harvested/immortalized (and will, hereafter, be referred to as; 'New Jerusalem'/the 'Kingdom of God'). The entire Earth has been set ablaze by the breath of God. All the dark angels have been (eternally) imprisoned in the Lake of Fire — along with the Devil, himself (and His Voice of Error/Evil). Now, **Rev 21:1-5** goes on, to say:

"*(1)* ***And I saw a new*** (restored) ***Heaven and a new Earth-***(flaming Morning Star)*:* ***for the first heaven*** (in crisis) ***and the first earth*** (corrupt/incomplete) ***were passed away; and there was no more sea-***(no more orb of ocean; Earth is now a flaming star). *(2)* ***And I John saw the holy city, new Jerusalem*** (the Kingdom of God; the Body of Christ)***, coming down from God out of Heaven, prepared as a Bride adorned for her husband*** (to perch atop the flaming morning star). *(3)* ***And I heard a great voice out of heaven saying, Behold, the Tabernacle of God is with men, and he will dwell with them, and they shall be his people, and God himself shall be with them, and be their God. (4) And God shall wipe away all tears from their eyes; and there shall be no more death,*** *neither sorrow, nor crying, neither shall there*

be any more pain: for the former

(corrupt/incomplete) *things are passed away. (5)*

And he that sat upon the throne said, Behold, I

make all things new. And he said unto me, Write:

for these Words are true and faithful." — (See;

Fig. 10[f] [pg. 281])

(**Rev 21:6-8** goes on, to say):

"(6) And he said unto me, it is done. I am Alpha

and Omega, the beginning and the end—(i.e.; the

First Word and the Last Word). *I will give unto*

him that is athirst of the fountain of the water

of life (Holy Spirit) *freely. (7) He that*

overcomes shall inherit all things; and I will be

his God, and he shall be my son. (8) But the

fearful, and unbelieving, and the abominable, and

murderers, and Whoremongers, and scorners, and

idolaters, and all liars, shall have their part

in the lake which burns with fire and brimstone:

which is the second death-(i.e.; eternal

prison)."

At this point in the Revelation, the angel begins

to describe the splendor of the Holy City (Kingdom of

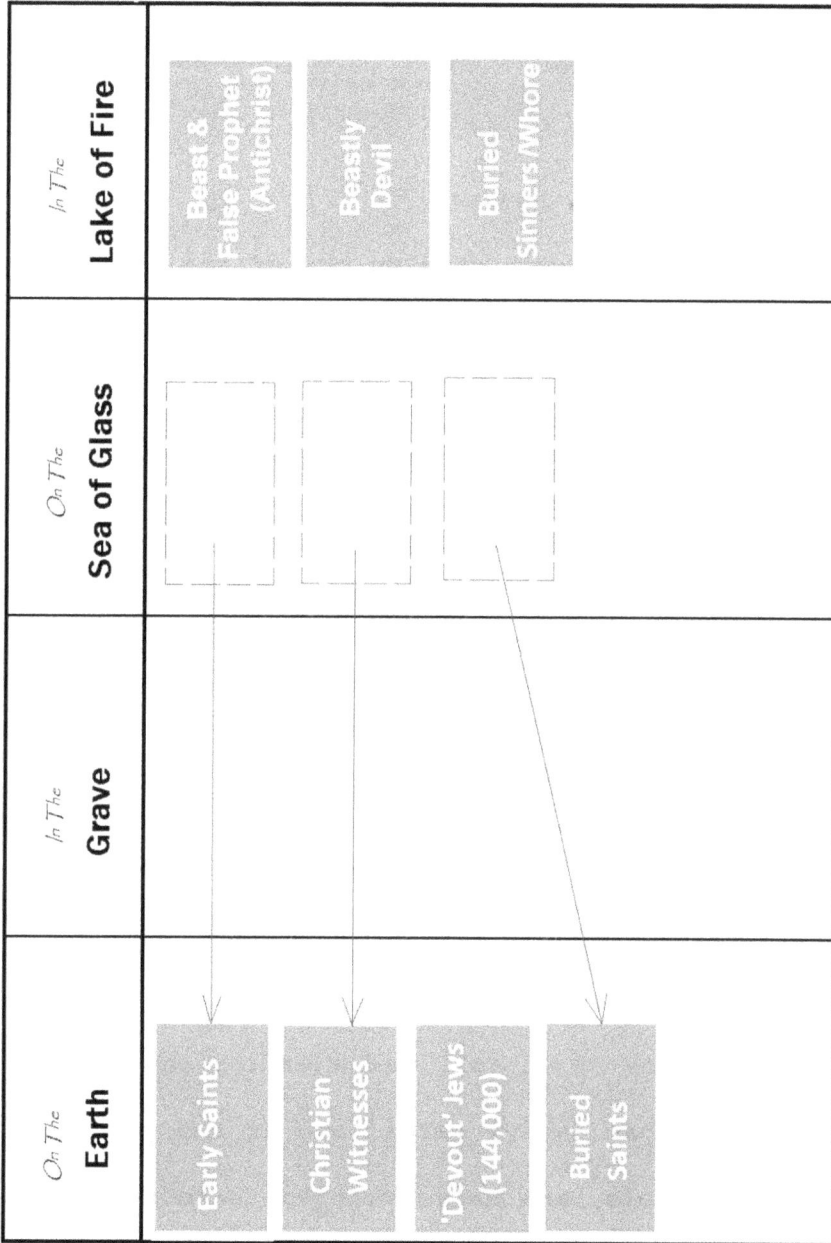

(Fig. 10f – All Resurrected Saints Inhabit the New Earth)

God) descending from God, out of Heaven; the

magnificent, jeweled, golden Body of Christ-(New

Jerusalem) finally coming to rest atop the flaming

Morning Star-(Lake of Fire). The beauty of this event

and the Holy City, itself, are so far beyond my artistic abilities that I won't even attempt to provide illustrations (I trust that I probably don't need to). **Rev 21:9-13** reads:

> "*(9)* ***And there came unto me one of the seven angels*** (of the Seven Churches) ***which had the seven vials full of the seven last plagues, and talked with me, saying, Come hither, I will shew you the Bride, the Lamb's wife. (10) And he carried me away in the spirit to a great and high mountain, and shewed me that great city, the Holy Jerusalem*** (the Kingdom of God; the Body of Christ), ***descending out of heaven from God, (11) Having the Glory of God: and her light was like unto a stone most precious, even like a jasper stone, clear as crystal; (12) And*** (the Kingdom/Body of Christ) ***had a wall great and high, and had twelve gates, and at the gates twelve angels, and names written thereon, which are the names of the twelve tribes of the children of Israel. (13) On the east three gates; on the north three gates; on the south three gates; and on the west three gates.***"

(**Rev 21:14-21** goes on, to say):

"*(14)* *And the wall of the city had twelve foundations, and in them the names of the twelve apostles of the Lamb.* *(15)* *And he that talked with me had a golden reed to measure the city, and the gates thereof, and the wall thereof.* *(16)* *And the city lies foursquare, and the length is as large as the breadth: and he measured the city with the reed, twelve thousand furlongs*—(i.e.; 1500 miles). *The length and the breadth and the height of it are equal* (a perfect cube)." *(17)* *And he measured the wall thereof, an hundred and forty and four cubits*—(i.e.; 216 feet), *according to the measure of a man, that is, of the angel.* *(18)* *And the building of the wall of it was of jasper: and the city was pure gold, like unto clear glass.* *(19)* *And the foundations of the wall of the city were garnished with all manner of precious stones. The first foundation was jasper; the second, sapphire; the third, a chalcedony; the fourth, an emerald;* *(20)* *The fifth, sardonyx; the sixth, sardius; the seventh, chrysolite; the eighth, beryl; the ninth, a topaz; the tenth, a chrysoprasus; the eleventh, a jacinth; the twelfth, an amethyst. (21) And the twelve gates were twelve pearls; every several gate was of one pearl: and the street of the city was pure gold, as it were transparent glass."*

(**Rev 21:22-27** goes on, to say):

"(22) And I saw no temple therein: for the Lord God almighty and the Lamb are the temple of it. (23) And the city had no need of the sun, neither of the moon, to shine in it: for the Glory of God did lighten it, and the Lamb is the light thereof. (24) And the nations of them which are saved shall walk in the light of it: and the kings of the earth do bring their Glory and honor into it. (25) And the gates of it shall not be shut at all by day: for there shall be no night there. (26) And they-(the kings) *shall bring the glory and honor of the nations into it. (27) And there shall in no wise enter into it any thing that defiles, neither whatsoever works abomination, or maketh a lie: but they which are written in the Lamb's Book of Life."*

(**Rev 22:1-5** goes on, to say):

"(1) And he shewed me a pure river of Water of Life, clear as crystal, proceeding out of the throne of God and of the Lamb. (2) In the midst of the street of it, and on either side of the river, was there the Tree of Life (Mind of Christ)*, which bare twelve manner of fruits, and yielded her fruit every month: and the leaves of the tree were for the healing of the nations. (3) And there shall be no more curse: but the throne of God and of the Lamb shall be in it; and his servants shall serve him. (4) And they shall see his face; and his name shall be in their foreheads. (5) And there shall be no night there; and they need no candle, neither light of the sun; for the Lord God gives them light: and they shall reign for ever and ever."*

Consider the following Old Testament Prophecy that discusses the New Jerusalem:

(Ref: Isa 65:17-25)—"(17) For, behold, I create new heavens and a new Earth: and the former shall not be remembered, nor come into mind. (18) But be ye glad and rejoice forever in that which I create: for, behold, I create Jerusalem a

rejoicing, and her people a joy. (19) And I will rejoice in Jerusalem, and joy in my people: and the voice of weeping shall be no more heard in her, nor the voice of crying. (20) There shall be no more thence an infant of days, nor an old man that hath not filled his days: for the child shall die an hundred years old; but the sinner being an hundred years old shall be accursed— (i.e.; in the Lake of Fire). *(21) And they shall build houses, and inhabit them; and they shall plant vineyards, and eat the fruit of them. (22) They shall not build, and another inhabit; they shall not plant, and another eat: for as the days of a tree are the days of my people, and mine elect shall long enjoy the work of their hands. (23) They shall not labor in vain, nor bring forth for trouble; for they are the seed of the blessed of the Lord, and their offspring with them. (24) And it shall come to pass, that before they call, I will answer; and while they are yet speaking, I will hear. (25) The wolf and the lamb shall feed together, and the lion shall eat straw like the bullock: and dust-*(ash) *shall be the*

Serpent's meat. They shall not hurt nor destroy

in all my holy mountain, says the Lord."

(**Rev 22:6-13** goes on, to say):

"(6) **And he**-(one of the seven angels with the

Seven Vials of the Seven Plagues of Wrath) *said*

unto me, These sayings are faithful and true: and

the Lord God of the holy prophets sent his angel

to shew unto his servants the things which must

shortly be done. (7) Behold, I come quickly:

blessed is he that keeps the sayings of the

prophecy of this book (the 'Revelation of John').

(8) **And I John saw these things, and heard them.**

And when I had heard and seen, I fell down to

worship before the feet of the angel which shewed

me these things. (9) Then says he unto me, See

you do it not: for I am your fellowservant, and

of your brethren the prophets, and of them which

keep the sayings of this book: worship God. (10)

And he says unto me, seal not the sayings of the

prophecy of this book: for the time is at hand.

(11) He that is unjust, let him be unjust still:

and he which is filthy, let him be filthy still:

and he that is righteous, let him be righteous

still: and he that is holy, let him be holy still. (12) And, behold, I come quickly; and my reward is with me, to give every man according as his work shall be. (13) I am Alpha and Omega, the beginning and the end, the first (Word) *and the last* (Word)*."*

(**Rev 22:14-21** goes on, to say):

"(14) blessed are they that do his commandments, that they may have right to the tree of life, and may enter in through the gates into the city.

(15) For without (outside the Kingdom of God) *are dogs, and sorcerers, and Whoremongers, and murderers, and idolaters, and whosoever loves and maketh a lie* (burning, in the Lake of Fire)*. (16) I Jesus have sent mine angel to testify unto you these things in the churches. I am the root and the offspring of David, and the bright and morning star. (17) And the Spirit and the Bride-*(Godly souls) *say, Come. And let him that hears say, Come. And let him that is athirst come. And whosoever will, let him take the water of life* (Holy Spirit) *freely. (18) For I testify unto every man that hears the Words of the prophecy of*

this book, If any man shall add unto these things, God shall add unto him the plagues that are written in this book. (19) And if any man shall take away from the Words of the book of this prophecy, God shall take away his part out of the book of life, and out of the holy city, and from the things which are written in this book. (20) He which testifies these things says, Surely I come quickly. Amen. Even so, come, Lord Jesus. (21) The grace of our Lord Jesus Christ be with you all. Amen."

Your eternal salvation can be won right now; today. If you have even the tiniest seed of faith — and even the smallest desire for the goodness of Jesus Christ to be 'true' — just open your mouth and ask Jesus to come into your heart; to reveal himself to you, to wash you in his blood, to teach you his Word, and to rule over and through you for the rest of your life. You will be welcomed, by legions of angels, into the Kingdom of God!

END

APPENDIX A – REVELATION GRID KEY

KEY: Revelation of John GRID:

Blocks 1-31	Blocks 32-62	Blocks 63-93	Blocks 94-124	Blocks 125-155	Blocks 156-186
I 1: 1-8 1: 9-11 1: 12-13	32	63	94	125	156
2 1: 14-16 1: 17-20 2: 1-7	33	64	95	126	157
3 2: 8-11 2: 12-17 2: 18-21	34	65	96	127	158
4 2: 22-29 3: 1-6	35	66	97	128	159
5 3: 7-9 3: 10-13 3: 14-22	36	67	98	129	160
6 4: 1-5 4: 6-11	37	68	99	130	161
7 5: 1-5 5: 6-9 5: 10-14	38	69	100	131	162
8 6: 1-2 6: 3-4 6: 5-6 6: 7-8	39	70 12: 1-4 12: 5	101	132	163

SCHEDULE of EVENTS:

*(Introduction)
   Risen Jesus speaks to John–(son of Zebedee).
   He appeared, holding the seven stars of the
   seven golden candlesticks which stand before
   him–(the seven angels of the seven churches
   on earth). He has a message for them–(us)...

* (God's ASSESSMENT of the 7 Churches...and His advise, to them)

      The Seven 'SCHOOLS-of-THOUGHT'...on earth:
(Ephesus)–More focused on 'the battle' than 'loving/saving'
(Smyrna)–-Struggling to hold faith [while bound under rebuke]
(Perga)–---Think to 'fight battle' from WITHIN Satan's lair
(Thya)–----Passively allows adultery/idolatry to be taught, near
(Sardis)–-Saved...but no motivation to SERVE God
(Phila)–--- Saved...and SERVING God–[strength, thru Jesus]
(Laod)–---- 'Lukewarm'–(trusting in selves; not God or devil)

* (PREVIEW of Scenario before the White Throne of God)

* (BOOK of 7 SEALS is introduced)
   This book lays out the purpose and timeline of
   everything in the history and destiny of 'mankind'...
   from beginning to end...

1st SEAL   (White Horse; ADAM'S ROLE)
2nd SEAL   (Red Horse; SERPANT'S ROLE)
3rd SEAL   (Black Horse; ISRAEL'S ROLE)
4th SEAL   (Pale Horse; JESUS' ROLE–['finished'])

HISTORICAL - PERIOD

Appendix A -- (Pg. 1 of 6)

KEY: Revelation of John GRID *(Cont.)* *SCHEDULE of EVENTS* *(Cont.)*

					Description	Category
9 6: 9-11	40	71 12: 6	102	133	164	**5th SEAL** (1st Resurrected SOULS; under Alter.) *(The rest of God's people are LEFT scattered in the WILDERNESS of ungodly mankind, until the end-times.)	EARLY HARVEST
10 6: 12-17	41	72 12: 7-10 12: 11-12 12: 13-17	103	134	165	**6th SEAL** (Dragon & 'Legion' are BANNISHED to Earth.) *(Devil LASHES OUT at mankind.)	AGE of GRACE
						TIME ELAPSES---2,000+ years will pass by	
11 7: 1-3 7: 4-8 7: 9-10 7: 11-12	42 11: 1-2	73	104	135	166	*(Jesus IDENTIFIES [and 'SEALS'] God's people): *(144,000 devout JEWS are 'SEALED' for heaven... [they WILL BE 'awakened' to Jesus by the Rapture events].) *(Innumerable 'SEALED' non-Jewish MULTITUDES are also IDENTIFIED.) *(JUSTIFICATION of the 'NON-Jew' MULTITUDES.)	PAUSE, in HEAVEN
12 7: 13-17	43	74	105	136	167	*(HOW/WHY the WHITE ROBES are AWARDED.)	
8: 1-6 8: 7 8: 8-9	44	75	106	137	168	**7th SEAL** (7 TRUMPS are issued into the earth.): *(Saints PRAYERS are cast into earth, with FIRE from the ALTER of God.) **1st TRUMP** (HAIL/FIRE/BLOOD; 3rd Part ofTREES/GRASS are burnt up.) **2nd TRUMP** (FIERY MOUNTAIN; 3rd part of SEA dies.) **3rd TRUMP** (WORMWOOD; 3rd Part of Rivers are poisoned.) **4th TRUMP** (3rd Part SUN/MOON/STAR-light is DIMMED.) *(Three 'WOE's' are coming):	POWER-UP PERIOD
13 8: 10-11 8: 12 8: 13							

Appendix A -- (Pg. 2 of 6)

KEY: Revelation of John GRID *(Cont.)* SCHEDULE of EVENTS *(Cont.)*

WARNINGS to the 144,000   **CHRISTIAN WITNESSES HARVEST**   **RISING of ANTICHRIST**

5th TRUMP 1st 'WOE': (ANGEL opens Pit; releasing the BEAST):
* (BEAST-['LEGION' of Error/Evil] FILLS the earth.)
* (ANTICHRIST-[VOICE of Error/Evil] RISES to power over this 3.5-yr period.)
* (During this SAME 3.5-yr period; TWO WITNESSES-[Christian church] are 'empowered' by God, against the ungodly.)
* (The BEAST OPRESSES mankind; stirring them up like a wasp nest. In the Last 5 MTHS, BEAST-['Legion' of Error] and ANTICHRIST-[Authoritative VOICE of Error] torture the UNGODLY...but they have NO POWER over the SAINTS DURING this time, because the SAINTS have been EMPOWERED against the enemy.)

6th TRUMP 2nd 'WOE': (TWO WITNESSES are KILLED by the by the BEAST/'LEGION'):
* (The earth is made DESOLATE of 'Holy' people/POWER, until the 144,000 are 'awakened' to Jesus, 3 days later.)
* (ANTICHRIST-[VOICE of ERROR] begins DEMANDING conformity; FREE-REIGN of ANTICHRIST, begins.)

* (HARVEST of the TWO WITNESSES-[the Christian Church]):
* (The 144,000/Remnant are 'AWAKENED' (to Jesus).)
* (RAISED Witnesses [on Sea of Glass] begin MINISTERING the GOSPEL to the 144,000/Remnant [on earth], from this point forward, throughout the 7 Last Plagues and the 1,000-yr reign.)

* (No one else will REPENT, from this point forward)

7th TRUMP 7 THUNDERS -- (Precursor to 7th Trump; the Secret Message)
* (The 144,000/Remnant are WARNED to FLEE Babylon.)
* (The GOSPEL[of Jesus] will be their ONLY STRENGTH.)
* (Escape SOUNDS sweet...but, the MEANS will not be.)

SORROWS - PERIOD -- (3.5-Years)

Col 1	Col 2	Col 3	Col 4	Col 5	Col 6
9: 1-4					
14 9: 5-8	*45* 11: 3-5	*76* 13: 1-3 / 13: 4-6	107	138	169
9: 9-12					
9: 13-15	*46* 11: 7	*77* 13: 7-10 / 13: 11-12 / 13: 13-14 / 13: 15-18	108	139	170
15 9: 16-17	*47* 11: 8-10 / 11: 11-13	*78* 14: 1-2	*109* 14: 14-16	*140* 15: 2-4	171
16 9: 18-19	*48* 11: 14-16	*79* 14: 3-5	110	141	172
17 9: 20-21	*49* 11: 17-18	*80* 14: 6-7 / 14: 8-11 / 14: 12-13	111	142	*173* 18: 1-2 / 18: 3-7
18 10: 1-3	*50*	*81*	112	143	174
19 10: 4-7 / 10: 8-9					
10: 10-11					

Appendix A -- (Pg. 3 of 6)

KEY: Revelation of John GRID (Cont.) SCHEDULE of EVENTS (Cont.)

MARRIAGE SUPPER

PLAGUES of WRATH

144,000 HARVEST

*(Heaven tells us HOW MUCH the LUKEWARM world will MISS the Great Whore, when she's destroyed.)

*(The 'SAVED' MULTITUDES [in heaven] celebrate the JOY of finally being 'AVENGED'.)

*(The MARRIAGE SUPPER of the LAMB takes place)

*(TEMPLE is OPENED...JESUS' ARMY is dispatched into the earth):
7th TRUMP 3rd 'WOE': (7 LAST PLAGUES, unleashed.)

1st PLAGUE (Noisome SORES [on UNGODLY].)
2nd PLAGUE (Sea Life DIES.)
3rd PLAGUE (Rivers/Fountains become BLOOD.)
4th PLAGUE (Man is SCORCHED with HEAT.)
5th PLAGUE (DARKNESS & PAIN prevail.)
6th PLAGUE (Euphrates DRIES...Battle of ARMAGEDDON occurs.)

7th PLAGUE ('WHORE' souls are destroyed.)
*(BEAST-(Legion of Error) and ANTICHRIST-(VOICE of Error) are CAST into Lake of Fire.)
*(The 144,000 [Remnant] are SLAIN/'CHANGED'-[harvested'.)

TRIBULATIONS - PERIOD -- (3.5-Years)

					Verses
20	51	82	113	144	18: 8-13
					18: 14-19
					18: 20-24
21	52	83	114	145	19: 1-6
					19: 7-10
		11: 19			
					19: 11-13
		14: 17-18			19: 14-16
		14: 19-20 & 15: 1			
22	53	84	115	146	15: 5-8
					16: 1-2
					16: 3
					16: 4-7
					16: 8-9
					16: 10-11
					16: 12-13
23	54	85	116	147	177
					16: 14-16
					16: 17-18
					178
					19: 17-19
					19: 20
24	55	86	117	148	19: 21
					16: 19-21
					179

Appendix A -- (Pg. 4 of 6)

KEY: Revelation of John GRID (Cont.)   SCHEDULE of EVENTS (Cont.)

1,000-YEAR REIGN

JUDGEMENT of DAMNED

* (Jesus tells John the MYSTERY of the GREAT 'WHORE'--- from beginning to end.)

* (Dragon is CAST INTO PIT ... and 1,000-YR REIGN BEGINS.)

TIME ELAPSES--1,000 years will pass by

* (Satan is LOOSED from the Pit.)
  * (LUKEWARM mankind is seduced/mustered against Christ's reign...only to be devoured with flame from Heaven.)
  * (Satan is CAST INTO LAKE of FIRE [forever].)

* (White Throne JUDGMENT [of the resurrected 'DAMNED'].)

* (Death & Hell are CAST INTO LAKE of FIRE.)

* (New JERUSALEM descends upon earth.)

* (New JERUSALEM is DESCRIBED.)

17: 1-6				
149 — 17: 7-8 / 17: 9-13 / 17: 14	118	87	56	25
150 — 17: 15-18	119	88	57	26
180				
181 — 20: 1-3 / 20: 4				
151	120	89	58	27
182 — 20: 5-6 / 20: 7-8 / 20: 9-10				
152 — 183 — 20: 11-12 / 20: 13-15	121	90	59	28
153 — 184 — 21: 1-5 / 21: 6-8 / 21: 9-13 / 21: 14-21	122	91	60	29

Appendix A -- (Pg. 5 of 6)

KEY: _Revelation of John GRID_ (Cont.) | **SCHEDULE of EVENTS** (Cont.)

30	61	92	123	154	185
					21: 22-27
					22: 1-5
					22: 6-13
31	62	93	124	155	186
					22: 14-21

* (TREE of LIFE)

*(Closing instruction to John and the Churches.)

Appendix A -- (Pg. 6 of 6)